Hearing the Voices of Jonestown

Religion and Politics
Michael Barkun, *Series Editor*

Hearing the Voices of Jonestown

Mary McCormick Maaga

With a Foreword by
Catherine Wessinger

Syracuse University Press

First Edition 1998

98 99 00 01 02 03   6 5 4 3 2 1

The paper used in this publication meets the minimum requirements of
American National Standard for Information Sciences—Permanence of
Paper for Printed Library Materials, ANSI Z39.48-1984. ∞™

Library of Congress Cataloging-in-Publication Data
Maaga, Mary McCormick.
Hearing the voices of Jonestown / Mary McCormick Maaga ; with a
foreword by Catherine Wessinger. — 1st ed.
p.   cm. — (Religion and politics)
Includes bibliographical references and index.
ISBN 0-8156-0515-3 (alk. paper)
1. Jonestown Mass Suicide, Jonestown, Guyana, 1978.   2. Peoples
Temple.   3. Jonestown (Guyana)—Religion.   I. Title.   II. Series.
BP605.P46M22   1998
289.9—dc21   97-45194

Manufactured in the United States of America

Dedicated to my husband, Boikanyo,
with love and gratitude
and to our son, John Desmond Tutu,
with love and hope

Amandla!

Mary McCormick Maaga is pastor of the United Methodist Church, Sergeantsville, New Jersey. She earned her doctor of philosophy degree with distinction from Drew University where she was invited to serve as the Shirley Sugarman Scholar in Religion and Society. In 1978 she was working for the mayor of Sacramento, California, when news was broadcasted that Congressman Leo Ryan had been murdered at Jonestown, Guyana. This experience was the beginning of her personal interest in the tragedy of Jonestown.

Contents

Foreword

CATHERINE WESSINGER

*E*veryone knows what happened at Jonestown. In 1978, Jonestown was a compound in the jungles of Guyana where over nine hundred brainwashed Americans lived. They were members of a church named Peoples Temple led by an insane, megalomaniac messiah, Jim Jones. After an unwelcome investigative visit by Congressman Leo Ryan, news reporters, and concerned relatives, which prompted some of the residents to defect, Jonestown men opened fire on Ryan's departing party killing five people including Ryan. Then the men returned to Jonestown where they joined the other residents in drinking punch laced with cyanide and tranquilizers. Some people were injected with the deadly potion. The children were killed first. People who did not want to commit suicide were forced to do so at gunpoint. Since no sane person would follow a leader so obviously delusional as Jim Jones, we can be certain that the Jonestown residents were brainwashed zombies. Further proof that Jim Jones had a controlling, narcissistic personality is the fact that he sexually exploited the women, and some of the men. The decision to commit murder and mass suicide was made by Jim Jones alone. Jones exercised total control over his followers. Jim Jones is solely to blame for the 922 deaths in Guyana on 18 November 1978.

The Jonestown myth is at once frightening and reassuring. It is frightening because, as we are warned by anticultists, anyone can be brainwashed by an unscrupulous religious leader. It is reassuring, because the Jonestown residents were clearly not in their right minds, since they were obviously subjected to mind control by Jim Jones. We can rest assured that sane people capable of making rational choices do not choose to kill others, their children, and themselves. Furthermore, we do not have to think about all the people of Jonestown— the 260 children, the seniors, the young people, the mature adults. The focus on laying all the blame on Jim Jones makes these people disappear. We do not have to confront them as individuals, who were committed to an ideal, and who possessed the ability to agree with and carry out the murder/suicide plan, and who also had the power to disagree and refuse to carry out those actions. Finally, we can be reassured that the residents of Jonestown were totally unlike ordinary, sane people like ourselves.

Mary McCormick Maaga asserts that the Jonestown residents are the "most intimate other," because they were human beings possessing agency, the ability to decide right and wrong, and they shared characteristics with ourselves. By attending to the voices of the Jonestown residents, who have been ignored due to the focus on Jim Jones, Maaga has found evidence that contradicts the received myth about Jonestown. The reality of Jonestown is more complex than what anticultists and the media have led us to believe. Jonestown had both good and bad features. Its residents were active in making the decision to carry out the mass murder/suicide, especially the young college-educated white women in Jim Jones's inner circle. Maaga questions the patriarchal assumptions that have been made about Jim Jones's "mistresses," and she listens to their voices. According to their testimony, through their relationships with Jim Jones, these young women found themselves empowered to actively improve the world and achieve concrete results involving social justice. These women loved Jim Jones, but they loved the cause even more. For reasons described by Maaga, the power of Jim Jones in fact declined in Peoples Temple after he left California for Jonestown. Jonestown documents demonstrate that the residents participated in making the decision to commit mass suicide if enemies threatened their collective, but the young women leaders and key men were most involved in making and facilitating that decision.

Religious commitment involves having an "ultimate concern," a goal that is the most important thing in the world for the believers (Baird 1971, 18). People may change their ultimate goals at different points in their lives, but sometimes individuals and groups may be so committed to an ultimate concern that they are willing to kill or die for it, or to do both. Early Christian martyrs are revered for dying for their faith, but today in America, we usually regard such people as fanatics, not as saints and heroes. The residents of Jonestown died in order to preserve their ultimate concern, their loyalty to each other as members of a socialist collective. Their ultimate concern was to preserve the unity of their community at all costs.

Although Jim Jones rejected the Bible, he articulated his teachings in the idiom of Protestant and Pentecostal Christianity. He termed his doctrine "apostolic socialism." Peoples Temple members were attempting to live out Jesus' injunction to love and care for the poor, the sick, and the downtrodden. Jonestown was a multiracial community committed to overcoming racism, sexism, ageism, and to helping everyone in need who came their way. They had withdrawn to Jonestown in Guyana as a refuge where they would be safe during the imminent apocalypse that would destroy the old sinful capitalist world and clear the way for communists to make a new world upholding human dignity and justice.

I have suggested that we use the term "catastrophic millennialism" for this ancient vision of the old world being violently swept away so that a collective salvation, a millennial kingdom, can be constructed (Wessinger 1997). A noteworthy feature of catastrophic millennialism is its dualism. Dualism is a perspective that divides reality into good vs. evil, us vs. them. A dualistic way of looking at the world is not only a common characteristic of "cultists," but also of "ordinary" people.

The Jonestown residents and the anticultists who opposed them were locked in a war fed by the dualistic worldviews of the participants on both sides. The anticultists were successful in enlisting the cooperation of federal agencies and officials, the media, and thereby public opinion in their project to destroy Jonestown. This degree of "cultural opposition" (Hall 1995) happened to occur at a time when Jonestown was suffering from internal weaknesses, including some caused by Jim Jones himself.

As demonstrated by Maaga, the combination of stresses internal to Jonestown—which by themselves threatened the ultimate concern —with the pressure from external opponents, precipitated the extreme actions on 18 November 1978. Most Jonestown residents agreed that their ultimate concern was worth killing and dying for. The transcript of the last Jonestown meeting (see app. B) provides evidence of peer pressure, persuasion, psychological coercion—by the whole group, not solely by Jim Jones—but there is no evidence that physical force was used to make people commit suicide.* As Jones said to Christine Miller, anyone could run who did not want to participate in the suicide, and some adults did. Other residents departed earlier because they knew the community had discussed and prepared for a mass suicide. The agency of adults in deciding whether they would or would not participate in the mass suicide/murder belies the brainwashing theory. Those who did kill others and/or committed suicide did so in order to preserve their ultimate concern.

Mary McCormick Maaga highlights the unheard voices of Jonestown and reveals the humanity and likeness to us of the Jonestown residents. In doing so, she elucidates the complex dynamics that produced so many deaths on that fateful day in Guyana. Let us hope that the mistakes of these fervent believers and the mistakes of their equally fervent opponents will not be repeated. Reciprocal demonization produces only violence and death, not life.

---

* I am saying that contrary to the media myth, we have no *evidence* that there was any physical coercion to join the mass suicide. The witnesses are dead. There is testimony of surviving witnesses of people willingly going to participate in the mass suicide. Certainly the children did not choose to die. Probably a number of elderly people did not have a choice. Dissidents in Jonestown were drugged and kept confined. These people did not choose to die. Able-bodied people could have escaped the suicide easily, and some chose to do so. My primary point here is that mass suicide could not have been carried out without the agency of the able-bodied adults.

Preface

*I*t was two years after meeting Reverend John and Barbara Moore before I learned that their daughters, Carolyn and Annie, had died at Jonestown. In those two years I was mentored by John and Barbara into the Christian life. Christian discipleship for them included an emphasis on people marginalized by mainstream society. John preached about the Kingdom of God and the justice embodied in Jesus Christ. Barbara mirrored this message in the diverse community she created in their home by offering accommodation and hospitality to runaways, prisoners, drug addicts, and people of every nationality and ethnicity. Both were, and are, activists on the front lines of social justice. I knew that their daughters had died tragically, but I thought that it had been in a traffic accident. Because they had discussed Jonestown so publicly—John had preached the Sunday after the tragedy (see app. C) and their daughter, Becky, and her husband, Mac, had written several books on Peoples Temple—they assumed that I knew.

I was shocked to learn how Carolyn Moore Layton and Annie Moore had died because of the conflict between my experience with the Moores and what I had read about the people who died at Jonestown. No daughter of John and Barbara was likely to have been brainwashed. I knew the depth of religious commitment that they had inspired in me and wondered what it would have been like to have been raised in their home and where that might have led me: to Peoples Temple, to Jonestown, to revolutionary suicide? Everywhere I turned for information I was confronted by a portrait of Carolyn as Jim Jones's mistress and little more. I set out to disprove this one-dimensional picture of my friends' daughter. What began as a very personal search for a deeper understanding of Carolyn has broadened to include a critique of that field of study which seeks to explain the behavior of people in new religions.

Because of my relationship with the Moores, I had the opportunity to meet Stephan Jones and Grace Stoen Jones, whose interviews with me added depth and detail to this study. On 18 November 1992 I went to the Jonestown Memorial Service at Evergreen Cemetery in Oakland, California, with John, Barbara, and Becky Moore, and Mary Sawyer, a friend of the Moores since the tragedy. I had never been to the service before, but John and Barbara go yearly. John told me that none of the "key players" show up at the service, which is organized by a consortium of black churches and people who lost relatives at Jonestown. A few reporters were milling around. CNN interviewed John and Barbara. By the time the service was scheduled to begin nearly two dozen people had arrived, mostly black. I was standing next to John when I looked at his face and saw that he was shaken. Then he said, "My God, it's Stephan." I followed his gaze and saw a tall, handsome man kneeling down next to the grave marker with a plant. He looked like Jim Jones, only taller, in better physical condition, and with a ponytail. A chill ran through me as Stephan made eye contact with John and walked toward him. They embraced, and John burst into tears, saying, "Stephan." Barbara greeted him, then he hugged Mary Sawyer, who said something to him about knowing his mother's sister. He turned to me and embraced me. John introduced me as a family friend, like one of their daughters. I said that I had written Stephan, but had not heard back. He asked at what address, and we clarified that he had moved recently. He gave me his new address and phone number and said that I could contact him.

Stephan then looked up the hill and saw Becky a little way off. Barbara started to say, "That's our daughter," but Stephan interrupted her and said, "I know, she looks just like Kimo" (the Moores' grandson by Carolyn and Jim Jones). John wept more heavily and was shaken while Barbara stood stiff and self-contained. Later, I asked her if she was okay, and she said, "I'll be okay because if I let myself start to fall apart I will never come back together again." Two white women arrived shortly after this conversation, and John told me he thought the petite one was Grace Stoen, whose son, John Victor, had been at the center of a child custody battle with Peoples Temple. During an impromptu lunch arrangement after the service I rode to the restaurant with Grace, who agreed to be interviewed by me at a later date.

What follows is my offering to Jonestown scholarship and to Carolyn and Annie.

Acknowledgments

*B*eing credited with the authorship of a book conceals an important truth—that a research project is produced by a community. This project was only feasible with the support of many people. My research at the Peoples Temple Archives of the California Historical Society during the winter of 1992 would not have been possible without the assistance of Jeffrey Barr, then library director, and the friendliness of Robert and George, who cheered me during some very long days of reading through documents. Stephan Jones gave multiple hours of interviews, which have been invaluable. I am grateful to Stephan for his time and for the offer of friendship that he and his wife, Kristi, extended to my husband, Boikanyo, and me. Grace Stoen Jones taught me a great deal about the inner workings of Peoples Temple and also how to embrace joy in the midst of grief and loss.

During the summer of 1995 I was encouraged through exhilarating and, sometimes, frustrating days of writing by the good humor and secretarial support of Yvonne McClymont and the warm collegiality of Murray MacBeath. Susan Sinclair spent several weeks during one of the hottest summers in Scottish history transcribing an audio tape of the suicide meeting. She also proofread much of my draft. Luke O'Curry spent painstaking hours collating the demographics. Throughout the two years of my tenure at the University of Stirling, my colleagues and students were unflagging in their enthusiasm for this project. Their encouragement, especially that of Jennifer Haswell, was essential to my creative process. In the past several years I have benefited greatly from the counsel and advice of Catherine Wessinger, former chair of the New Religious Movements group of the American

Academy of Religion, whose own work on new religious movements and women in religion has inspired me.

Then there are those people whose influence on one's life transcends any individual project. Karen McCarthy Brown has taught me what I know about being a scholar, including how to live in the ambiguity of what one learns and to embrace it. Bob Coote has taught me how to fan curiosity into investigative fire. Diane Du Brule Siebert has taught me how to stay sane throughout all of life's challenges, including the research and writing of this book. Her loving and ever-mirthful support of me and this project included the preparation of the manuscript for publication during an especially busy time in my life. Without Diane's help I would not have been able to balance motherhood, ministry, and my scholarly work while getting this book into print. Thank you, Diane.

I would not have undertaken an investigation of Peoples Temple without the blessing of John, Barbara, and Becky Moore. I thank them for trusting me.

Even with this abundance of technical support, practical help, encouragement, advice, and blessings I would not have been able to "live" with Peoples Temple and Jonestown in the way that I have for the past seven years without the loving and thoroughly genuine passion of my husband for me and this project. How can "thank you" sound anything but trite in reference to a man whose dedication to our creative partnership and marriage is the reason that the following book exists?

Introduction

*J*onestown is more than a place in Guyana where an American religious group lived and died. Jonestown has come to symbolize the worst possible outcome of religious commitment. Since 1978, whenever there is violence in a nonmainstream religious group, such as the Branch Davidians, Solar Temple, or Heaven's Gate, comparisons are made with Peoples Temple and the deaths that occurred at Jonestown. This book grows, in part, out of my frustration with these comparisons.

Peoples Temple was an attempt by its founder and participants to create an egalitarian society in which hierarchies based upon race, class, and gender would be erased. The groups to which Peoples Temple is frequently compared had no such aspirations. The horrific end to Peoples Temple grew out of a combination of both its success and failure in creating a community based upon Christian and socialist ideals. Its success meant that the individuals who joined Peoples Temple came to see each other as family and their community as a model for addressing the racism and classism of America. Its failure was mirrored in a leadership structure that was almost exclusively white and college educated and largely female, whereas the membership was predominantly black and either skilled or unskilled laborers. For the leadership elite at Jonestown the symbolic importance of what had been created in Peoples Temple began to be more important than the individual lives involved. As pressure built from relatives, former members, politicians, and the news media for Jonestown to be disbanded, this combination of family loyalty and elitist decision making merged to create an environment in which suicide was embraced as the only option in which community, albeit in the spiritual realm, and ideological purity could be maintained.

Jonestown was a unique religious phenomenon. The decision to commit suicide was a singular response to a complex set of communal pressures. I do not believe that any universal lessons about religion or charismatic leadership can be learned from Jonestown in spite of the photos of the Jonestown dead that are televised every time a group makes a radical and deadly step in the name of religious commitment. Because of the horror that took place on 18 November 1978, much that was positive in Peoples Temple, not to mention the individual personalities who dedicated their lives to its radical understanding of society, has been erased. This book is an attempt to restore the humanity of the individuals who were a part of Peoples Temple. For this reason the details of the history, organization, and personalities of Peoples Temple are highlighted. The reward for the careful reader will be a greater understanding of why adults in the Jonestown community chose to take their lives.

For this process of reconstructing the life and times of Peoples Temple to be most effective it has been necessary to engage in the scholarly task of deconstructing many existing analyses of Jonestown. It may be tempting to skip chapter 2 in which I discuss the theories and methods that have informed scholarly and popular conclusions about Jonestown, but the voices of Peoples Temple can only be heard once the misunderstandings are left behind. Although chapter 2 is theoretically denser than any that follow, it is the foundation upon which my theory is built.

Much work remains to understand the complex religious, political, and personal dynamics at work in Peoples Temple. This book is my attempt to initiate the next wave of Jonestown scholarship.

Hearing the Voices of Jonestown

1

Who Were the Members
of Peoples Temple?

*I*n contemporary religious studies there is "before Jonestown" and "after Jonestown." The deaths of more than nine hundred people in a jungle commune, the vast majority of whom died by ingesting a cyanide-laced beverage, signaled the end of an era of relative religious tolerance in America and the beginning of a time of cynicism, paranoia, and fear about nonmainstream religions, variously referred to as cults, sects, alternate religions or new religious movements. Although Sun Myung Moon's Unification Church had been much in the news and the courts before November 1978, the widespread belief in new religions as irredeemably dangerous was not a feature of Western culture until Jonestown. Jonestown has become a watchword for the madness of charismatic leadership, the vulnerability of religious devotees, and the dangers of experimenting with religion outside the mainstream American religious institutions. Even those scholars and commentators who defend the right of people to choose nonmainstream religious groups generally accept the portrait of Peoples Temple as an example of the danger of too great a commitment to religious ideology as embodied in the person of a charismatic leader. The tragedy of Jim Jones and Peoples Temple, for even the most tolerant observer, demonstrates the proclivity for bizarre and dangerous behavior that most (if not all) new religions possess.

I elucidate the historical and sociological particularities of Peoples Temple and Jonestown to undercut the simplistic way in which "Jonestown" has been used to bring other nonmainstream religions into question. Before 1978 the Peoples Temple was not featured in the anticult literature; for the remainder of the 1970s and well into the

1

1980s it was difficult to find a page, let alone an issue, of a magazine or newsletter published by the anticult lobby that did not contain at least one (frequently several) references to the mass suicide/murder (Barker 1986, 330). By understanding Peoples Temple and the socio-logical dynamics that contributed toward its tragic end, one gains an appreciation for the power of religious ideology, political commitment, and the alchemy of love, loyalty, and rebellion that is intrinsic to communal living situations. My goal in this study is *not* to develop a universal theory about the potential for violence within new religions but to make the violence that occurred in this particular religious group more understandable.

In 1954 Jim Jones rented a building in Indianapolis and began his own church—Community Unity—after a frustrating experience as a student pastor at the Somerset Southside Methodist Church. His pri-mary reason for leaving the Methodist Church was a dispute with the leadership over interracial worship (Hall 1987, 17). Jones and Marceline Baldwin, who were married in 1949, bought a building in 1955 and moved the newly named Wings of Deliverance Church there. Later that year the name was changed to the Peoples Temple Full Gospel Church, an affiliate of the Disciples of Christ denomina-tion. In 1961 Jim Jones received his bachelor's degree in education from Butler University and was appointed to the Human Rights Com-mission in Indianapolis. After several years of intensive ministry in Indianapolis, Jones and his family traveled to Brazil where they stayed until 1963. When they returned from their travels, Jones announced to his congregation that his family would be moving to Redwood Valley, California. He encouraged the members of Peoples Temple to relocate with him. His choice of Redwood Valley was based upon a January 1962 *Esquire Magazine* list of the safest places to be in the event of a nuclear war. In 1964 Jones was ordained a minister in the Disciples of Christ denomination.

In the summer of 1965 Jones and Peoples Temple moved to Red-wood Valley, California, with approximately 70 members of the Indi-ana sect. Numbers vary as to how many traveled with Jones from Indiana. No official membership records were kept by Peoples Temple at the time of the move to California, so scholars have estimated anywhere from 40 to 140, based on the number of Hoosiers who ended up at Jonestown; it was probably about 70, because few members were gained in Redwood Valley between their arrival and the first official membership records in California. By 1966 the Temple had 86 members and by 1967, 106, according to Disciples of Christ membership records (Moore 1985, 112). Beginning in 1968 a new type of member began to join Peoples Temple: young, educated, white. In 1969, after several years of meeting in rented buildings, Peoples Temple was able to build a church of their own in Redwood Valley, which the group named Happy Acres. The number of members grew exponentially once Peoples Temple expanded its ministry to the urban blacks of San Francisco and Los Angeles, opening churches in 1970 and 1972, respectively.

In 1972 a baby was born, John Victor Stoen, whose paternity would be at the center of the maelstrom that would lead Congressman Leo Ryan to investigate the community Peoples Temple had established in Guyana, South America. The year 1972 was also when the first critical stories came out in the press, most notably those by Reverend Lester Kinsolving published in the *San Francisco Examiner*. In these articles Kinsolving ridiculed claims by members that Jones was able to raise people from the dead and pointed out the presence of armed guards at Temple services. Peoples Temple responded by flooding the *Examiner* with letters of complaint against Kinsolving and by picketing outside the newspaper's office with accusations that the newspaper was against religion. The significance of these articles lay not so much in the reaction provoked from Peoples Temple as in the encouragement and public platform they gave to disaffected members and others opposed to the Temple (Hall 1987, 114–15).

The transition to Guyana began in 1974 when a small group of Peoples Temple members rented a house in Georgetown and as "pioneers" began clearing the land. By 1975 fifty people were stationed at "Jonestown" and most of the rest of the Temple had relocated from Redwood Valley to San Francisco. For the next two years Peoples Temple was deeply involved in San Francisco political activities, and the group was instrumental in electing George Moscone to the office of mayor. As demonstrated in the Kinsolving conflict, Peoples Temple was always able to mobilize large numbers of people for any cause the Temple leaders identified as significant. In return Jim Jones was appointed to the San Francisco Housing Authority.

By May 1977 there were still only about fifty members of Peoples Temple at Jonestown, but by the following September that number had leaped to more than one thousand residents. Jones relocated to Jonestown in July 1977, apparently in response to a damaging *New West Magazine* exposé based upon interviews with former members that alleged physical, sexual, and financial abuse within the movement. From summer 1977 until November 1978 there were increasingly vitriolic exchanges between the residents of Jonestown and a group—Concerned Relatives—which was attempting to expose Peoples Temple and Jones as a dangerous "cult." Concerned Relatives included family members of residents of Jonestown and former members. Jeannie and Al Mills (a.k.a. Deanna and Elmer Mertle), former members of Peoples Temple who defected in October 1975, and their Human Freedom Center were at the heart of the Concerned Relatives organization. Later, Steve Katsaris, the father of inner circle member Maria Katsaris, became very active in Concerned Relatives. Particularly vehement in his opposition to Jones and Jonestown was Timothy Oliver Stoen, whose love and devotion to Jones while a member had turned to hate after leaving the movement in June 1977. He and his former wife, Grace Stoen, initiated legal action to gain custody of their son, John Victor, who lived at Jonestown.

By September 1977 the tension and stress at Jonestown was mounting as a result of the combination of a large dependent population—more than half of the residents at Jonestown were either children or senior citizens (see appendix A, table 1)—and the stress of reacting to the legal actions and negative media coverage initiated by Concerned Relatives. As fear, paranoia, and hopelessness gained ascendancy at Jonestown, the plan for "revolutionary suicide"—an idea that had been spoken about and practiced as a ritual of loyalty within the leadership circle of Peoples Temple since 1973—began to take shape.

Congressman Leo Ryan, well known for his attraction to political issues that would draw media attention, was courted by Concerned Relatives to become their champion in their duel with Peoples Temple. Ryan had spent a day as a teacher in Watts in the 1960s and a day as an inmate at Folsom prison; both were portrayed by him as investigations into conditions and both had received widespread and favorable news coverage. Ryan had already heard of Peoples Temple through a constituent, Robert Houston, who first registered concern with the congressman about the involvement of his son in spring 1977. In October 1978, several months after Debbie Layton Blakey's high-profile defection and accusations of potential suicide at Jonestown, Ryan wrote to the chair of the International Relations Committee of the United States Congress to ask official permission to go to Jonestown.

The details of the events that led to the deaths of nearly one thousand people seem banal enough, yet they conceal a complexity that is the focus of this study. On 1 November 1978 Congressman Leo Ryan sent a letter to Reverend Jim Jones requesting a visit to Jonestown. A petition signed by the residents of Jonestown who objected to the visit was delivered to Ryan on 9 November. Nevertheless, the Ryan delegation left from New York on Tuesday, 14 November, destination Georgetown, Guyana. Ryan's delegation included two congressional staff members, two reporters, and a news photographer from San Francisco, four journalists from NBC, including a camera crew, a freelance writer, and fourteen members of the Concerned Relatives group, including Grace and Tim Stoen. On 16 November, Congressman Ryan called Jonestown a "prison" before actually seeing it. The next day the two Peoples Temple lawyers, Mark Lane and Charles Garry, met with Ryan and later that day persuaded Jim Jones to let Ryan and a delegation come to Jonestown. By 4:30 P.M. on Friday, 17 November, Congressman Ryan, his assistant, Jackie Speier, all eight news representatives, and four members of Concerned Relatives arrived with Lane and Garry at Jonestown. They were met at the gate by Marceline Jones, Jim Jones's wife, and given a formal tour, entertainment, and a meal. At 11:00 P.M. that night a note was handed to Don Harris, the NBC correspondent, reading: "Vernon Gosney and Monica Bagby. Please help us get out of Jonestown" (Reiterman and Jacobs 1982, 503).

The next day, Saturday, 18 November, Ryan completed his planned interviews, and Harris disclosed to Jim Jones that some people wanted to leave. Another fourteen people came forward and asked to leave with the Ryan delegation, most of them from two families who had been longtime members of the Temple, the Parks and the Bogues. Then a knife attack on Ryan by Temple member Don Sly left only a superficial wound but had a chilling effect on the delegation and community. Larry Layton, former husband of Carolyn Moore Layton and brother of Temple defector Debbie Layton Blakey, claimed he wanted to defect with the other sixteen and joined them on the truck that was leaving for the Port Kaituma airstrip. While the delegation and defectors attempted to board the planes, several men who had followed the delegation on trucks from Jonestown opened fire. Shortly thereafter, around 6:00 P.M., the suicides at Jonestown began.

There were 923 deaths directly related to the events in Guyana on 18 November 1978. Five people were shot to death at the Port

Kaituma airstrip who were part of Congressman Leo Ryan's returning entourage: Ryan; 3 journalists, including NBC correspondent Don Harris, his cameraman Bob Brown, and *San Francisco Examiner* photographer Greg Robinson; and Patty Parks, a member of a family that had been part of Peoples Temple since its Indiana days who had decided to leave Jonestown with Ryan. Ten people were wounded at the airstrip. There were 911 poisonings at Jonestown, 260 of them children. Because autopsies were not widely performed on the Jonestown dead, it is not known how many ingested the cyanide laced Fla-Vor-Aid, how many were injected, nor indeed, whether some died of gunshot wounds or other causes. Only 7 bodies were autopsied of the 917 Peoples Temple dead: Carolyn Moore Layton, Ann Elizabeth Moore, Jim Jones, Dr. Larry Schacht, Maria Katsaris, Richard Castillo, and Violet Dillard (Moore 1988). What is known for certain is that there were two obvious deaths from gunshot wounds: Jim Jones and Annie Moore, a nurse at Jonestown whose sister, Carolyn Moore Layton, was in the leadership of Peoples Temple. David Chidester states that 3 were shot at Jonestown although he offers no proof of the identity of the third person (Chidester 1988b, 161). Jonathan Smith asserts that 4 died of gunshot wounds and that 70 individuals "showed puncture wounds which suggest that they were injected with poison" although there are no autopsy results to substantiate this claim (J. Z. Smith 1982, 108). In Georgetown, Guyana, Sharon Amos, a Temple loyalist from the early California days, slit her own throat and those of her 3 children. Four months after the deaths of the 922, Temple inner-circle member Mike Prokes shot himself in the head after calling a press conference at which he released a forty-page document, attempting to clarify the mission of the religious movement and to explain the decision of Peoples Temple to commit "revolutionary suicide."

Eighty-five people survived the suicide-murders of 18 November, including Hyacinth Thrash, a seventy-six year-old member who slept through the entire event. Several families and individuals escaped into the jungle and the members of the Jonestown basketball team, including two of Jim and Marceline Jones's sons, were in Georgetown playing in a tournament against the local Guyanese team.

Jonestown as a physical site was a miracle of construction and dedication, a fact that is not widely appreciated when one only sees it in photographs with dead bodies strewn about. A total of 3,824 acres was leased from the Guyanese government for the "Peoples Temple

Agricultural Mission." Three hundred of those acres were cleared by fewer than fifty colonists using the clear-cut and burn method. Stephan Jones, the only biological son of Jim and Marceline Jones, went to Guyana in February 1977 and was part of the group that created the town where jungle once reigned. Half of the people who built Jonestown were urban California youths sent to Jonestown because they had disciplinary problems, and half were "tough Midwestern blue-collar workers who knew how to use their hands" (Wright 1993, 67). In an interview with me Stephan Jones spoke of the pride that the pioneers had in the construction of Jonestown. Many of these urban youths had never built anything before in their lives, and simply seeing the town become a reality was motivation enough for the group to work sixteen or eighteen hours a day. There was freedom in Jonestown in those days, Jones reminisced besides self-imposed discipline. The pioneers worked long hours and ate frugal food, but they got to decide themselves when the workday ended and what they would do with their limited free time. This freedom changed once Jim Jones and his leadership team arrived and "began systematizing the work, monopolizing all the free time, and speaking on the loudspeaker system all the time" (Stephan G. Jones interview, 11 Dec. 1992). Stephan Jones and the other pioneers especially resented the well-educated elite who introduced committees that "second-guessed" the work of the manual laborers (Reiterman 1982, 348).

The pioneers built sixty cottages designed to house eight people each, and five single-sex dorms. After the influx of immigrants in the summer and fall of 1977, these residences were filled beyond capacity. They also constructed a communal kitchen and pantry, drying sheds for food, an infirmary and drug dispensary, an office and radio room, a laundry area, two school buildings, and a nursery and preschool. A large open-sided pavilion was constructed so that the entire town would have a place to gather for meals, community meetings (called the Peoples Rally or Peoples Forum), entertainment and worship. Finally, two large cabins were constructed for the use of Jim Jones and his leadership circle.

Life at Jonestown after the fall of 1977 was difficult. The mission had not been designed to provide for such numbers. Every adult had a bed, but some children had to share. Like most communes, the settlement was developed with an emphasis on public space. Individual privacy was not a priority at Jonestown nor was free time (Hall 1987, 235–36). A typical day at Jonestown was filled with work, meetings, and public gatherings. Everyone who was able-bodied had a job at Jonestown, most working in agriculture, teaching, healthcare, or providing the daily needs of the community by preparing meals and washing up. The young went to school daily, and the elderly did not have to work at all although many did help with food preparation and gardening. Jones spent many hours of each day broadcasting news and commentary from his cabin over the Jonestown public address system. He was assisted in managing the community by a core group of leaders who coordinated committees and departments covering every aspect of life (236–37).

In the evenings Peoples Rallies were held in which socialist ideals were discussed and disciplinary problems were "brought up." Punishment for those who were not contributing enough to the life of the community usually involved assignment to work crews that cleaned the latrines or did other heavy and disagreeable work (Hall 1987, 240). These public meetings were also the forum for creating consensus within the community and for Jones to convey a sense of the special importance of the enterprise in which they were engaged. Occasionally, educational exercises were practiced in which people were asked to write about their understanding of socialist ideology and about their willingness to sacrifice for the survival of Jonestown.

The theology of Peoples Temple was a mix of the ethical teachings of Jesus with the social critique of Marx. Jones called this blend *apostolic socialism*. Of particular importance to Peoples Temple was Matt. 25:35–40, which was printed on their stationery and pamphlets. This passage reads in part: "For I was hungry and you gave me food, I was thirsty and you gave me something to drink, I was a stranger and you welcomed me, I was naked and you gave me clothing, I was sick and you took care of me, I was in prison and you visited me. . . . Truly I tell you, just as you did it to one of the least of these my brothers, you did it to me." Care for the marginalized in society, especially blacks and the elderly, was a central mandate of this theology as was communal living. Jones pointed out that the early followers of Jesus had lived communally, as stated in Acts 2:44–45: "All who believed were together and had all things in common; they would sell their possessions and goods and distribute the proceeds to all, as any had need." Apocalypticism and reincarnation were also threads in the Peoples Temple theology. Jones believed the end of the world would come about either through nuclear war or a fascist takeover (Moore 1985,

157). It was his fear of nuclear war that caused Jones to choose California as the site for the first Peoples Temple relocation. Guyana was to be the Promised Land of security and peace away from the corrupting influence of American society and the persecution of opponents. For Peoples Temple destruction of their community, if not the world, always loomed on the horizon. It is not clear whether Jones's belief in reincarnation was widely shared. A number of people from Indiana had joined from the spiritualist tradition, but most members of Peoples Temple were from mainstream Christian backgrounds. Carolyn Moore Layton informed her family in the early 1970s that Jim Jones and she were the reincarnation of Vladimir Lenin and his mistress (Moore 1986, 62). At the suicide meeting reincarnation was raised by both Jim Jones and Jim McElvane as each attempted to calm people once the dying had begun (see app. B).

Who were the Peoples Temple members who left America to move to Jonestown, Guyana? The demographics paint a portrait of a religious movement attempting to break down the barriers of age, race, and class. Three hundred forty of the nearly one thousand residents were nineteen years of age or under; nearly one hundred fifty people were sixty-six years or older, (see app. A, table 1.) Roughly half of the residents of Jonestown were dependent on the rest of the community as a result of youth or age (Moore 1985, 113). Jonestown was populated with representatives from thirty-nine of America's fifty states (Smith 1982, 108). Between 70 and 80 percent of the residents of Jonestown were black. Weightman represents the more liberal estimate of black population with 80 percent, whereas Reiterman estimates that 70 percent of Jonestown residents were black, 25 percent white, with the rest "a smattering of mulatto, Hispanic, American Indian and Asian" (Weightman 1983, 82; Reiterman 1982, 346). Nearly two-thirds of the residents were women (Reiterman 1982, 346). In the most thorough consideration of the race, age, and gender demographics to date Archie Smith points out that just fewer than one-half of the population of Jonestown were black women, most of them (14 percent) sixty-six years or older. His numbers demonstrate clearly the race and gender composition of the Peoples Temple community in Guyana: 49 percent black women; 22 percent black men; 14 percent white women; 10 percent white men (A. Smith 1982, figs. 1 and 2).

Why these people left California to live in a jungle commune in Guyana is a question with a variety of answers, depending upon which "kind" of member one is querying. Three groups were coexisting within Peoples Temple by the time it moved to Jonestown: the original members from Indiana (mostly white); the young, educated white members who joined after Peoples Temple relocated to Redwood Valley; and the members who joined once the ministry of Peoples Temple expanded into San Francisco and Los Angeles—elderly black women, women (mostly black) with children, and young black males. The organizational dynamics this combination of groups created are addressed in chapter 5. The mostly female leadership of Jonestown was drawn primarily from the California white professional group with important support from the Indiana members. The rank and file were almost exclusively urban blacks of all ages and both genders.

Most of what has been written about the members of Peoples Temple who moved to Jonestown and died there has focused on the utopian dreams of the white members who joined in the early California years and the socioeconomic needs of the blacks who became members during the Peoples Temple urban expansion. But this "white utopianism—black deprivation" split is not completely accurate and could be interpreted as both racist and classist, as Stanley Hauerwas has pointed out:

> One of the most disturbing aspects of reactions to Jonestown is the inherent racism and class prejudice implied. The assumption is that if these people had just been better educated and well off they would not have fallen for this kind of cheap and trashy religion. There is no empirical or moral basis, however, for such an assumption. (Levi, 1982, 191 n. 10)

In fact, a great deal of utopian desire motivated the urban blacks to follow Peoples Temple to the "Promised Land." Several months after the suicides, a black woman member who had not gone to Jonestown noted that Peoples Temple "provided the atmosphere of love, trust and social concern that she found lacking in other black institutions" (Chidester 1988b, 44). The journalist Lawrence Wright suggested that it was more the belief in the "promise of racial equality" than in food, shelter, and economic security that motivated the black senior citizens to join Peoples Temple and then move to Jonestown. These were people who had internalized Marcus Garvey's Back to Africa movement during the 1920s; almost half of the elderly residents of Jonestown had already migrated once from the American South to California in search of a more just society.

> The foundation of his [Jones's] ministry was a promise of racial equality. His followers had grown up in a racist society and suffered economic injustice, and, whether they came from a tenant farm in Mississippi or a cotton mill in Georgia, they had not found redemption in California. Jones made them believe that they could create it themselves—that they could make their own Paradise. (Wright 1993, 69)

This is not to say that there were not some black members who were attracted into Peoples Temple membership by economic and security considerations. Perhaps this is, in fact, a false dichotomy. It may only be Western assumptions about the nature of religion and philosophy that force a split between utopian ideology and economic considerations. After the suicides, Debbie Touchette, a young black woman whose father Archie Ijames had served as associate pastor with Jim Jones in Indiana, told Rebecca Moore: "My family lived on scraps from the garbage cans behind the A&P and Kroger's in Indianapolis. I was raised in Peoples Temple. No one will ever make me think that social change is brainwashing. Peoples Temple was really helping people" (Moore 1985, 78).

Elderly people who had lived in poverty and loneliness in San Francisco and Los Angeles were provided with superior health care and community through their affiliation with Peoples Temple. Most of the older adults (fifty-one to sixty-five years of age) and seniors (sixty-six and older), who made up one quarter of the population of Jonestown, joined Peoples Temple after 1970 when the Temple's ministry expanded into urban California. Of the older adults, nearly one-half (51 of 104) indicated a health problem on the forms they filled out for the Peoples Temple leadership in preparation for moving to Jonestown. Nearly 60 percent (85 of 146) of the seniors indicated a health problem. At Jonestown they were able to contribute to the life of the community according to their physical capabilities. As Reverend John Moore wrote after he and his wife, Barbara, visited Jonestown in May 1978: "I know of no retirement home which provides better food and health care and a more wholesome environment. They are part of a community with babies and children as well as of young people and adults. This fact is a two way street, benefiting the young as well as the old" (Moore 1985, 194). Stephan Jones emphasized this latter point as the primary attraction for everyone who was a member of Peoples Temple, no matter what her or his race, gender, class or educational attainments: the need for "a sense of belonging" (Jones interview, 25 May 1993).

I am not suggesting that the experience in Peoples Temple was the same for the educated whites and for the urban blacks. In fact, I argue quite the opposite in the chapters to come. What I am suggesting is that the difference between these two groups was not so much what motivated them to join Peoples Temple in the first place as were two factors that would contribute centrally to the events of November 1978: first, what each identified as the significance of the group once the pressure increased at Jonestown and second, the difference in their economic and social abilities to leave Jonestown. "Marginalization" in mainstream society for the white elite at Jonestown was exclusively affiliative. Once one of them chose to return to the middle class (or higher) lifestyle from which she or he came, then the marginalization that came with belonging to a religious group committed to racial integration would end. This was not the case for the majority of Jonestown residents, who would return to the United States only to face a continuation of racism, ageism, and classism. The significant defections from Jonestown that drove the decision to commit suicide were from the California leadership circle and the Indiana founding members. The black members of Peoples Temple did not have much to return to in urban California nor did they have the economic resources with which to make the transition once they had thrown in their lot with Jones and the Temple.

Thus, I have focused on the particularities of the people involved in Peoples Temple and, later in the analysis, on the specific people who defected at various times. It is not possible to understand what happened at Jonestown without "knowing" the people. As Mary Sawyer, who worked with members of Peoples Temple as an assistant to California Lieutenant Governor Mervyn Dymally, pointed out, "The trauma of Jonestown has vastly more meaning when the victims are known as real people who laughed and cried and worked and loved and dreamed great dreams" (Sawyer 1981). The failure of scholars to look more deeply than "70–80 percent black" or "two-thirds women" means that at some level the discipline of sociology of religion is subscribing to the belief that the commitment of these people to a new religious movement makes them somehow generic and interchangeable. Whereas scholars of new religions offer critiques of the "brainwashing theory" of Margaret Singer, in fact, much of what is written in the field shares an unspoken assumption with Singer that "we" are in our "right" minds and would never join such a group except from the safety of a participant-observation vantage point.

2

Deconstructing Jonestown

M uch of the work that has been done by scholars in the field of new religious movements has focused carefully and effectively on a fairly narrow range of concerns—the conversion and commitment of members and the charismatic powers of the leader—while using, almost exclusively, the method of participant observation. Although a number of interesting and well-researched pieces have resulted,[1] little has been attempted to forge new theoretical ground in the study of new religions. I challenge here the implicit assumptions of the theoretical framework that has been used to analyze Peoples Temple and, in so doing, suggest new ways of interpreting the data available. The scholarly method that most informs what follows is deconstruction. This two-step process involves both a critical evaluation of the underlying assumptions that frame what has been written about Jonestown and a challenge of those assumptions by asking questions from outside the predominate ideology of that frame. The conclusions I have drawn about Peoples Temple based on this method are surprising and unlike what has been written before.

A Survey of Jonestown Scholarship

Scholars of religion admit the difficulty of explaining what happened at Jonestown, Guyana, on 18 November 1978. In *Salvation and Suicide* David Chidester uses *structured empathy*, which he describes as "a curious combination of detached objectivity and empathic subjectivity" that "requires that we temporarily suspend prejudicial

1. Among the best are Barker 1984 and Carter 1990.

biases and value judgments in order to enter imaginatively into the worldview of others" (Chidester 1988b, xiv). Not surprisingly, given that sociological theories often reflect the methodology employed by the scholar, Chidester concludes that "collective suicide fused the worldview into a single act" (155). As Thomas Robbins has rightly pointed out, arguing that the "worldview" of Peoples Temple caused the suicides does not explain what happened at Jonestown because Chidester's construction of a universally held outlook on life is a somewhat static abstraction that is ahistorical (Robbins 1989, 34). In addition, Chidester fails to take into account the socioeconomic, educational, and racial diversity of the movement, which surely affected the way in which each member experienced, internalized, and expressed that worldview. Although it is among the most analytical treatments of Peoples Temple to date, Chidester, nonetheless, operates with the assumption that the movement acted as a group in its thinking and that its understanding of the world was derived primarily, if not exclusively, from Jim Jones. The former concept is a view that is common in Jonestown scholarship and derives in part from the image of the "mass" suicide in which the people are perceived to have acted in one accord and must, therefore, have been of one mind all along. In my view this is a more sophisticated version of the popular brainwashing theory. The latter concept—that the worldview and the organizational direction of Peoples Temple flowed from Jim Jones through his leadership circle and then to the members—is one of the assumptions that I challenge.

Judith Weightman's starting point with Peoples Temple is quite different from Chidester's although her conclusion is much the same. Rather than treat the members of Peoples Temple as a "mass," Weightman, in her book *Making Sense of the Jonestown Suicides* (1983), examines the racial and socioeconomic diversity of the group and then asks how such a diverse group could act collectively in committing "revolutionary suicide." Her method is an application of Weberian *verstehen*, which posits that social behavior can only be understood in terms of the "motives" of those who perform the actions. Like Chidester, she identifies Jones as holding the power in the group although her understanding of how that power functioned between Jones and the members is rather more sociologically sophisticated. According to Weightman, the ultimate power actually lay with the people, but since they bestowed Jones with authority and helped him to maintain it "Jones remained the central source of power in the

Temple" (208). Weightman identifies an elite of "young, attractive, white women" who were instrumental in implementing Jones's vision for the group and who were more loyal to Jim Jones than they were to the movement (208). "Initiation" into the leadership elite was accomplished through these young women having a sexual relationship with Jones (208). Weightman repeatedly links female power in Peoples Temple with sex in a way that narrowly defines and limits the kind of power that the women in the leadership of Peoples Temple exercised. This noncritical acceptance of a "natural" connection between gender and sex when women within a group are studied and the failure to address in any kind of nuanced way the power that was exercised by women in the leadership of Peoples Temple is another ideological schema that I deconstruct and examine.

For a purely sociohistorical point of view a student of Peoples Temple could scarcely do better than John Hall, *Gone from the Promised Land* (1987). He places the Temple's political, social, and religious activities in the context of 1960s and 1970s America in an effort to break down the barrier the suicides erected between mainstream society and the members of Peoples Temple. His research is painstaking as is his methodological self-consciousness. "Appendix: A Comment on Methodology," which follows his treatment of Jonestown, demonstrates his theoretical sophistication. He writes about using Max Weber's classic approach through four interrelated analytic frames: historical narrative, sociological analysis, causal historical analysis, and cultural interpretation (313–17). The question that drives his research is, "How much of what happened with Peoples Temple is unique to the group and its leader, and how much can be explained by reference to wider social processes?" (xviii). His interest is in "social forces," not in the internal dynamism of the group. In the end Hall concludes that it was the mix of apocalyptic religiosity and revolutionary politics combined with the pressure from ex-members and members' families that led to the suicides. In Hall's view mass suicide could never be a vehicle for victory for political revolutionaries, only for messianic-apocalyptic revolutionaries. Peoples Temple had already committed revolutionary suicide in a number of respects—by living communally and moving to Guyana—before their ultimate act. Hall concludes that, "they had died to anything but 'principle' long before" (304) and, therefore, the decision to take the cyanide flowed naturally from the political and religious stance they had embraced as a community all along. Because of the macroscopic view of events Hall takes, he misses the significance of the individuals involved in the decision to commit suicide.

A Survey of Scholarship on Women in New Religious Movements

The linking of women and sex, as though sex is located in the woman and not in the space between two people, is a frequent occurrence in the contemporary study of new religions in the West. Even in scholarly work that is otherwise quite innovative, gender roles and sexual behavior are generally treated together, the assumption being that if one is writing about women, then sexual behavior must be addressed as well. This is not so with men, who can be written about in their various social and leadership roles without mention of sex. Not only do males have no "sex," they also appear to have no "gender" in the same way that "whites" appear to have no "ethnicity." The article by Robbins and Bromley, which suggests that new religions are "laboratories of social experimentation," is an example of this assumption. They suggest that new religious movements challenge mainstream society in terms of "sexual-gender arrangements" and "patterns of economic resource mobilization" (Robbins and Bromley 1992, 1). Women's contributions to the "economic and organizational experimentation" of new religions are not mentioned at all although Peoples Temple is the focus of nearly one-third of the section. The centrality of women's leadership and participation in the social and economic experimentation of Peoples Temple should not have been invisible to the careful scholar. Robbins and Bromley are indeed careful scholars, so I can only conclude that their exclusion of the women in the leadership of Peoples Temple is the result of the constraints of the ideological framework they apply. Given this schema, it is only natural that women are the focus of their section on "sexual patterns and gender roles." The authors argue that the instability of gender roles in mainstream society has created a situation in which women are attracted to either new religions with traditional patriarchal expectations or feminist spiritual groups in which there is "equalitarian" participation and leadership (5–13).

Yet, in many ways, the inclusion of women as a focus for study in the literature on new religions, although frequently linked with sexuality, is an improvement over the erasure of women in the standard histories of American religion. As Mary Bednarowski pointed out in her foundational study of women's religious practice and leadership in nineteenth-century America, women are the "hidden ones" whose contributions to religion have either "gone largely unrecorded" or are marginalized as merely supportive of male religious leadership (Bednarowski 1980, 208). Bednarowski notes, "The women go to church and the men exercise the authority as members of the clergy and as professional theologians" (208). Many scholars have pointed out, although few with the critical sophistication of Bednarowski, that it is in the marginal or nonmainstream religions that women have found the theological and institutional freedom to exercise spiritual authority. Bednarowski's four-part analytic scheme for understanding the kinds of religious groups in which women are most likely to practice leadership has engendered several excellent essays that are included in *Women's Leadership in Marginal Religions: Explorations Outside the Mainstream* (Wessinger 1993). Like the work of Bednarowski, these studies have tended to focus on those movements in which a woman was the charismatic leader, namely, the Shakers (Ann Lee), the Christian Scientists (Mary Baker Eddy), and the Theosophists (Helena Blavatsky). Interest has also been shown in the role of women in the various Spiritualist groups that were popular during the nineteenth century in America.[2] Today there is great interest by scholars in Elizabeth Claire Prophet, who succeeded her husband, Mark Prophet, as the leader of the Montana-based Church Universal and Triumphant.

Another school of interest has focused on the three religious groups that are credited with the most gender role and sexual experimentation during the nineteenth century: the Shakers, Mormons, and Oneida Perfectionists. Most scholars who have studied these groups agree that the motive for both men and women's involvement was a desire to restructure the social disorder and gender ambiguity that was pervasive in America in the early nineteenth century (see Aidala 1985, 287; Foster 1981, 227; Kern 1981, 15–16, 312–13). Although these movements were viewed by mainstream society as being dangerously innovative, they were, in fact, deeply conservative attempts to subsume sexuality and women's power within a religious-utopian ideology. Even "free love" within the Oneida community is best understood as hyper-regulated communal love. Foster notes, "Although outsiders typically fantasized about the 'licentious' behavior that sup-

2. See Braude 1989 for an analysis of women's leadership in contemporary Spiritualist groups. See also Haywood 1983.

posedly went on in this 'free love' colony, in reality complex marriage at Oneida was associated with control mechanisms that might appear even more restrictive in some respects than Shaker celibacy. Romantic liaisons were systematically broken up; group criticism sessions dealt bluntly with any sexual behavior that did not conform to Community norms" (Foster 1981, 235). All three authors suggest that members of these new religions had a "low tolerance for ambiguity" (Aidala 1985, 287).

When female followers have been studied within contemporary new religions, there has been a tendency to focus on those groups in which "traditional" gender roles and male-female relationships are present. Janet Jacobs's analysis of the religious commitment of seventeen women to eight different "nontraditional" religious groups is representative of the concerns of this theoretical approach.

> The analysis suggests that in religious commitment an economy of love is operationalized in which the commodities of exchange are affection, approval, and intimacy. As such, the male religious hierarchy plays a significant role in the lives of female converts through control over the emotional rewards of religious commitment. Such control often leads to sexual exploitation, abuse, and discrimination, sources of female subordination that are reinforced by the pervasiveness of romantic ideals, expectations of male protection and love which come to dominate the interaction between the female devotee and the male leadership. (Jacobs 1984, 155)[3]

Although my research into Peoples Temple demonstrates that emotions, sex, and love were elements in the involvement of many women, it is clear that these were not separate motivational impulses from their desire to exercise leadership and to contribute to changing the world. My disagreement with Jacobs comes down to how she and I evaluate the social function of these relational experiences. The basis of my argument about the women in leadership of Peoples Temple, particularly Carolyn Layton, is that love for the male charismatic leader grew out of love for the movement. The basis of Jacobs's argument is that a woman's involvement in a new religious movement is a reflection of her unmet emotional and sexual needs, which she finds temporarily met in her involvement with the male charismatic leader.

3. See also Jacobs 1989.

Jacobs asserts that it is "the responsibility of the female devotees . . . to serve the male religious leaders in exchange for the rewards of emotional gratification" (Jacobs 1984, 156).

For Jacobs, the power in the movement flows from the male charismatic leader to the female followers, who are subject to subordination and abuse because of their emotionally vulnerable states of mind. Three assumptions about women in new religions undergird her work: first, that a woman who involves herself in a group with conservative "sex role socialization patterns" could not have intellectual or political reasons for doing so, but joins only because of a condition of emotional deprivation; second, that sex and romance are at the heart of the relationship between the male charismatic leader and his female followers; third, that all the power and authority in these groups is held by the male leader.[4] Although all of these assumptions may have been supported by the data in Jacobs's study (see below for the bias implicit in using only "apostates"—people who have left new religious movements—in one's study) her conclusion that "this analysis suggests that female religious commitment involves a love-centered economy in which conversion is experienced as an emotional exchange" (Jacobs 1984, 170) is a universal pronouncement that reflects a particular ideology, which, by virtue of its gendered parameters, does not allow for women (or male charismatic leaders) who do not fit within its framework of assumptions (for gendered ideology see chap. 3). I am not suggesting that affection and intimacy between a follower and leader is never the primary motivation for a woman to join a religious movement, only that Jacob's analysis maintains that this economy of love inevitably places the follower in a position to be exploited and abused. It is not clear to me whether this concentration of power in the hands of the charismatic leader actually derives from the data Jacobs collected or was implicit in the schema she applied.

As in Jacobs's work, Susan Palmer widens the scope of analysis without challenging the theoretical and methodological assumptions that undergird it. She offers students and scholars specific "insider" details about the variety of roles available to women in new religions through an application of this same ideological framework. She directly links women and sex at the outset of her investigation. One of

---

4. For a sociological analysis of some of the reasons why women embrace traditional gender roles, see Kaufman 1991; for a more personal analysis, see Ochs 1990; for a specific treatment of charismatic Christian women, see Susan Rose 1987.

her two standard questions when interviewing the women in the seven groups she investigated was, "Which social-sexual problems she [the member] sought to resolve by moving into a religious commune and what she hoped to leave behind" (Palmer 1994, xii).[5] Her theoretical framework not only assumes that women and sex are linked but that a woman must have "problems" that have driven her into the new religious movement. One wonders how different her results would have been had she conducted these interviews outside of the "sex-problem" framework. Like those who studied the Shakers, Mormons, and Oneida Perfectionists, Palmer concludes that women join marginal religions in response to "dramatic upheavals in the structure of society" that directly affect how they understand their role as women (xiii). Women desire a community that offers gender role clarity in a world that is "characterized by sexual freedom, gender confusion, family breakdown, and moral ambiguity" (xvii).

All these studies, whether focusing on the nineteenth or on the twentieth century, female charismatic leaders or members, broaden understanding of women's participation in new religions but do not challenge either the methods or theories employed in the study of religion. An implicit assumption remains that to study the leader is to understand the religion; to know the abstract formulations of the social confusion of an age is to understand the attraction of the religion to its members. Stripping these assumptions away, one discovers something quite different: a new theoretical framework leads to a different set of questions. A different set of questions leads to different results.

An Application of the Methods of Foucault and Smith

Foucault and Smith agree that scholarly inquiry must be guided by a search for the weaknesses of a theoretical construct. They also agree that those weaknesses are easiest to find where assumptions, rather than evidence, most heavily undergird conclusions. Foucault expresses it in the form of a wish: "I dream of the intellectual who

5. The book is the first in a Syracuse University Press series, Women and Gender in North American Religions, suggesting that the analysis of women's religiosity from an interdisciplinary, cross-cultural perspective is of increasing interest to scholars and students.

destroys evidence and generalities, the one who, in the inertias and constraints of the present time, locates and marks the weak points, the openings, the lines of force" (Foucault 1988, 124). Foucault has been my guide through the labyrinth of existing narratives about Peoples Temple. He cautions one to be suspicious of analytical packages that are too tightly wrapped.

> We must question those ready-made syntheses, those groupings that we normally accept before any examination, those links whose validity is recognized from the outset. . . . And instead of according them unqualified, spontaneous value, we must accept, in the name of methodological rigor, that, in the first instance, they concern only a population of dispersed events. (Foucault 1972, 22)

The idea that Jim Jones held all the power in Peoples Temple and that the women who were within the leadership circle of the movement were primarily there because they were in a sexual relationship with Jones are two such "ready-made syntheses." To go back to the "population of dispersed events" one must put to one side the conclusions that have already been reached by others and then listen carefully to the silence that remains. Chidester summarizes Foucault's method as an "archaeology of [the] silence" of those discourses which are excluded when a field narrows (Chidester 1986, 2).

Foucault reminds scholars to practice archaeology within their chosen disciplines: to dig, and in digging to uncover the framework of power and knowledge that constrains what they label "truth." Lawrence Kritzman has called this a "new form of social activism" in which intellectuals challenge the "institutional regime of the production of truth" (Foucault 1988, xviii-xix). I uncover here the outlines of this "production of truth" about Peoples Temple and Jonestown— the sticky web of assumptions about new religions, about women, about the relationship between sex and power in which Jonestown is caught.

Smith poses the issue in terms of a sociological method that intentionally listens for the voices that have been systematically silenced through application of the "discourses of power" (D. E. Smith 1987, 3). She writes about a "point of rupture" (49) that occurs when women practice sociology and discover that the experience of their gender has been largely ignored, marginalized, or misconstrued. The task of the feminist scholar is to identify the "gender subtext" of the theories that she employs. Women "outside the frame" (63) have an opportunity to evaluate sociological data in a new way, in a way that questions not only the results of the research that has been done but the methods that have been employed and the theoretical constructs that have determined what constitutes data. When sociological results consistently serve to shore up patriarchy—as the results of research into women in new religions surely do—then it is likely that the analysis is more dependent on the ideology undergirding the theoretical apparatus than on the data itself.

When applying Foucault and Smith to the case of Peoples Temple, I discovered what had been left out of the narratives that have been told about its history, namely, the particularities of the people who were members and, specifically, the exercise of power by the women in leadership. In what has been written to date Jim Jones is centrally located to the exclusion of the experience of many of the people—mostly women—who actually made Peoples Temple and Jonestown function day to day. The fact that women have been excluded—both by men and through their own complicity, as D. E. Smith points out (1987, 34)—from the "ideological work of society" has resulted in "a history constructed largely from the perspective of men, and largely about men" (35). This has certainly been the case in what has been written about Peoples Temple. What happens to the portrait of Jonestown when the women are restored to their positions of power and authority in the narrative? What happens when a "systematic consciousness of society and social relations from the standpoint of women" is adopted with regard to Peoples Temple (16)?

To reconstruct the Jonestown narrative with women restored to their positions of organizational and moral agency is not without risk. Part of the reason they have been marginalized and tightly contained within an ideological schema that limits their power is because their "heresy" in joining Peoples Temple and contributing toward the decisions that led it to its tragic end is too threatening to contemplate. It is better to keep the women as the blameless victims of a madman than to recognize them as participating in the destruction of an entire community. But then Chidester, reflecting on Foucault, reminds that "there is the tendency of any 'us' to dehumanize 'them'," in an effort to "create a sense of self by excluding others" (Chidester 1986, 7). What would happen to our sense of "self" as women, as religious practitioners, as seekers after social justice, as Americans, if we integrated the "them" of Jonestown into "us"?

Virginia Burrus has called heretics "the most intimate other" (1991, 2). Herein lies a tension that has colored our ability as scholars and citizens to understand people involved in new religions: because they are intimate they are threatening to "our" sense of who we are; because they are "other," they seem to bear no relation to who "we" are. The women in the leadership of Peoples Temple embody this tension of "the most intimate other." It is possible for me to recognize myself in their relentless and self-sacrificial search for justice and human decency. At the same time, it is almost impossible to see myself devising a plan to kill an entire community in a symbolic act of "revolutionary suicide." To bridge this heretical gap so that my intimacy with the women in leadership is maintained while their otherness is mitigated makes the Jonestown narrative more difficult to read and experience because it challenges the constructions of female power in new religions and, in so doing, makes the actions of the women in leadership understandable as the behavior of mature, politically and religiously motivated, human beings. In so doing I risk falling over the heretical edge. (This creates a kind of empathic dilemma for the scholar and student: Does understanding why humans engage in horrific behavior lead to a justification of it? Scholars such as Robert J. Lifton, whose work on the Nazi doctors has helped to make their barbaric actions "understandable" within their own psychological and sociological frame of reference, have encountered this dilemma. Here, as did Lifton, I explain but do not condone.)

An Evaluation of Primary Sources

Each of the various resources and sources I have used contributes its own particular perspective to the portrait. The documents held in the Peoples Temple archives at the California Historical Society, which were retrieved both from Jonestown and the San Francisco administrative offices of Peoples Temple, have given a sense of the bureaucratic complexity of the Temple as a religious, social, political, and economic organization. The documents of specific interest to me were written by residents at Jonestown.

All data available for an analysis of Peoples Temple are biased in one way or another. Defectors and the Concerned Relatives told "atrocity" stories. Residents of Jonestown wrote letters and educational assignments deeply influenced by the isolation of their community and the information they were receiving from their leaders. The media were sensationalist. The U.S. government was and is selective about the information it makes available. Survivors and sympathetic family members are emotionally scarred from their losses. Most journalists and many scholars have discounted any material written by Peoples Temple members as biased beyond use because of the assumption that the residents of Jonestown were the victims of mind control. (See chapter 3 for the allegations of brainwashing.)

An accurate evaluation of the available first-person narratives about Peoples Temple depends upon an understanding of the psychosocial dynamics at work when people write or speak about their experiences in a new religious movement. When individuals rejoin mainstream society after leaving a new religion, former members must explain their previous commitment in a way that will help them be accepted back into families and communities. Most people who leave a new religion after having made a serious commitment to it defect with very little money and few friends outside the movement. The goal for the apostate is to reenter mainstream society with relatively few emotional and social penalties.[6] The narratives generated in this psychosocial process of reintegration share certain particulars that "explain" the estrangement of former members from their families: food and sleep deprivation; chanting, frequent prayer, unrelenting harangues from the charismatic leader; threats to people's safety if they should leave the group. All of these "cult" practices allegedly contribute to the "brainwashing" of the person who had been a member. The public, the media, and some scholars subscribe to the belief that these "atrocity" narratives reflect "the truth" about what goes on inside new religions and that anyone who has something positive to say about their experience as a member of a new religion must still be under the power of the "cult's brainwashing, mind-control technique." As Bromley, Shupe, and Ventimiglia point out, however:

> The intent of such tales is not to present the complexity of events dispassionately but rather . . . to make the event and individual stand out from the ordinary. Each contestant in this struggle to define reality will portray events as he or she sees them or wishes others to see them. Whether such stories represent some kernel of

6. Shupe and Bromley have explored this process of "apostates" telling "atrocity stories" in several of their jointly written articles and books, most notably in Shupe and Bromley 1980, 1981. See also Bromley and Richardson 1983.

"truth" is not only difficult to validate in many cases but is also irrelevant. The stories gain their persuasiveness and motivating power from their larger-than-life quality. (1979, 43–44)

The "truth," then, of a narrative such as Debbie Blakey's affidavit, in which she alleged that widespread physical, financial, and psychological abuse was taking place at Jonestown was in Blakey's belief that self-destruction by the group was at hand and that attention needed to be drawn to that possibility (Steve Rose 1979, 168–75). The truthfulness of her specific charges are more a question of perspective than of accuracy. In article 9 of her affidavit Blakey wrote, "Rev. Jones insisted that Temple members work long hours and completely give up all semblance of a personal life." What may have looked like an appropriate exertion of physical effort to an "insider" may, on reflection, appear to be unfair work demands to a newly received "outsider." This switch in perspective is decidedly more likely when the "apostate" is being counseled by those who believe that a lack of privacy and physical labor are necessary components of a mind-control strategy. The Reverend John Moore, who visited Jonestown with his wife Barbara the same week that Blakey defected, wrote upon his return: "The two words that came to my mind immediately as I was there [at Jonestown], and as I tried to reflect upon my experiences, were "impressive" and "amazing." It almost boggles the mind to see that great clearing, and to understand how so much could have been done in the relatively short period of time" (Moore 1985, 264). The communal nature of Jonestown could scarcely have come as a surprise to Blakey, who had been a member of Peoples Temple since 1971. The emphasis on the group over the individual had always been a part of Peoples Temple philosophy and social organization (Moore 1985, 261). Blakey was drawing attention to the hard work and lack of personal space with an awareness of how this would sound to people who were skeptical about the motives of people who would involve themselves in a communal living arrangement in the first place.

Still, drawing attention to the meta-narrative of atrocity tales does not discount the validity of much of what was being said by former members about Jonestown. Because of what happened on 18 November and the understandable unwillingness of any family to admit or believe that their loved one participated "in sound mind" in the poisoning deaths of nearly three hundred children, the brainwashing argument is especially compelling. What happened at Jonestown seems beyond what any rational individual, let alone more than nine hundred individuals, would ever do. *Time* magazine in the fortnight after the tragedy reflected the most frequent explanatory tone based on the atrocity stories of former members and journalistic conjecture: "In an appalling demonstration of the way in which a charismatic leader can bend the minds of his followers with a devilish blend of professed altruism and psychological tyranny, some 900 members of the California-based Peoples Temple died in a self-imposed ritual of mass suicide and murder" (Geline 1978, 16). Although this kind of explanation protects readers from any sense of connection with the people involved and, thus, saves them from subsequent experiences of grief, guilt, or complicity, it does not explain what happened and why.

Narratives that portray Peoples Temple as having been a relentless horror are overstating the case as much as are the narratives—much less frequently publicized by the media or used by scholars—that argue that Jonestown was a paradise before conspirators and traitors set out to destroy it. Both reflect views that are tightly organized around a core ideological imperative. Apostates emphasize the negative to reintegrate into mainstream society. Loyalists emphasize the positive to reaffirm the commitment they have made to the new religion.[7] Both kinds of narratives contain elements of truth and untruth. Part of my method in researching Jonestown has been to weigh more heavily those narratives that have been marginalized or erased as a result of an assumption of brainwashing by those who have heretofore written about Peoples Temple. A careful reading of these materials written at Jonestown demonstrates the complexity of the social dynamics at work in the community. The individual struggles and motivations of the people involved are also visible. These letters were written for Jim Jones or others in the community and were not composed to glorify Peoples Temple to the outside world. When compared to the narratives of the apostates and loyalists, they look authentic, containing the ambiguities, longings, and conflicts of life in a highly populated community.

To identify the ideological schema that frames each narrative—whether written by an apostate or a loyalist—and to weigh the "truth" of what has been said and written in light of that schema one must take seriously the writings of anti-cult and Concerned Relatives activ-

7. For more details about how this reaffirmation of loyalty contributed toward the decision to commit suicide, see chapter 7.

ists, but instead of giving specific credence to the charges of brainwashing and coercion, look for what they have to say about issues, such as organizational structures and ministry practices, which were less ideologically bounded. In the same way, as one reads the letters and educational assignments from people who were resident at Jonestown, one analyzes the histrionic denunciations of traitors and pledges for revenge, not in terms of the mind-set of the individual writer but in terms of what those narratives overall had to say about the stress level of the community and the larger organizational and leadership issues being considered at the time.

Demonization of the opposition was practiced by both Concerned Relatives and Peoples Temple. Each labeled the other as the embodiment of chaos and evil. Concerned Relatives accused Peoples Temple of brainwashing their children and labeled them a cult. Peoples Temple accused Concerned Relatives of attempting to destroy their community and labeled them fascist. From a sociopsychological point of view demonization was a useful practice for both groups, for it provided Concerned Relatives and Peoples Temple with feelings of control and empowerment while suggesting that any blame or wrongdoing lay entirely with the "enemy" group. The power that Concerned Relatives and Peoples Temple exercised, however, was not equal. Because Concerned Relatives were closer to the "relations of ruling," as Dorothy Smith (1990) would have it, than was Peoples Temple, they were able to mobilize the political and social resources of mainstream society. Concerned Relatives' ideological schema became the lens through which the media and Congressman Ryan came to understand Jonestown.

For both groups the combination of aggression and self-righteousness, which is at the heart of demonization as a social practice, was a heady mixture that perpetuated itself until both groups could conceive of no way out of the conflict other than the utter destruction of the enemy. Richardson, Best, and Bromley (1991) collected articles by scholars from a variety of disciplines to examine the construction of "satanism" as the most recent (and in some sense, ultimate) example of demonization in American culture. Ironically, although demonization appeared to empower the group that was blaming and pointing fingers, it, in fact, disempowered that group because it placed all the ability to harm in the hands of its opponents. The vast degree of power concentrated in the demonized group is more apparent when one examines the seven characteristics that are frequently ascribed to demonized groups: all-powerful; well-orchestrated; secretive; harmless looking on the outside; require specialists to uncover the evil of the group; pervasive; and the innocent in the group and in society are the most in danger. Demonizing accusations raise the stakes of the conflict and make the differentiation between an "insider" and an "outsider" paramount. The most dangerous person of all, once demonization is in place, is the traitor; the one who looks like an "insider" but is, in fact, an "outsider." The demonization of Concerned Relatives and those who had left Jonestown resulted in an environment that made defection and the freedom that it would provide impossible.

Several letters written by Ann Elizabeth Moore during her sojourn at Jonestown elucidate the probable thinking of the Peoples Temple inner circle and the mood of the Jonestown community. Moore herself was only a peripheral member of the Jonestown elite. The best proof of this is that there were letters from her to Jim Jones among the papers retrieved from Jonestown. I discovered no letters discussing substantive issues from Carolyn Moore Layton, Maria Katsaris, Teri Buford, Debbie Layton Blakey, Harriet Tropp, Mike Prokes, or Stephan Jones, all people widely considered to be part of the Jonestown "aristocracy." I assume that my failure to discover written documents authored by them indicates they were able to talk with Jones daily and did not need to write. Although not a member of the inner circle, Ann Moore was, nonetheless, privy to much that went on within the highest organizational echelons of Jonestown. She was Jim Jones's personal nurse at Jonestown, and her older sister, Carolyn Moore Layton, was one of the chief administrators of the Peoples Temple community.

Besides letters from individuals, scores of documents at the California Historical Society reveal the bureaucratic depth and range of the Peoples Temple ministry. The Schubert Hall Library of the California Historical Society maintains the Peoples Temple archives. The archive comprises three collections of documents: MS3800, 130 boxes of documents compiled by the receiver of the Peoples Temple estate after the tragedy; these records constitute the remains of the bureaucratic organization of the San Francisco and Los Angeles branches of Peoples Temple; MS3801, 12 boxes of documents taken from Jonestown, Guyana, by the U.S. government; the Moore Family Collection, 5 boxes of letters, photos, sermons, journals, and reflections written by the parents and sister of Carolyn Moore Layton and Ann Elizabeth

Moore. Recently, Stephan Gandhi Jones gave the California Historical Society many of his photographs and other personal items related
to Peoples Temple.[8] The materials written at Jonestown during the fall
and winter of 1977 and 1978 documented the creation of a model
socialist community. Great effort poured into the organization of the
school system, health care provisions, agricultural plans, community-
wide socialist education, and so forth. Clearly, the individuals who
designed these strategies for community success were not doing so just
for themselves (which would have needed far less documentation)
rather they were doing so for other groups, or, perhaps, for posterity, as
a reference for how such a community was to be run. A kind of
optimism pervades these documents. During the spring, summer, and
fall of 1978 the focus of these general, anonymous, administrative
papers turns from internal to external concerns: the custody battle for
John Victor Stoen; the defection of Debbie Blakey; the activities of
Concerned Relatives; the negative press coverage from the United
States; potential problems, deriving from all these, with the Guyanese
government; and, finally, objections to a visit from Congressman Leo
Ryan.

Multiple interviews with Grace Stoen and Stephan Gandhi Jones
helped clarify a number of specific issues and revealed the emotional
intensity of life in Peoples Temple, an aspect missing in most of what
has been written about Jonestown and an important factor in understanding the decision to commit suicide.[9]

I focus on Carolyn Moore Layton in chapters 3 and 4 because she
embodies the tension between the gendered ideological schema within
interpretations of Jonestown and the reality of life in Peoples Temple.
She was both a leader in the Peoples Temple movement and the lover
of Jim Jones as evidenced in the primary documentation, including
FBI interviews, Peoples Temple internal reports, letters and memoran-
dums, the letters that Layton wrote to her family while she was in
Peoples Temple and living at Jonestown, and interviews with people

8. References to manuscripts from MS3800 and MS3801 are cited hereafter as
CHS followed by the document number.

9. Stephan Jones, Jim and Marceline Jones' son, gave me nine hours of interviews plus access to photos from Jonestown. Grace Stoen Jones, a Peoples Temple
member who defected in 1976 and whose son, John Victor Stoen, was at the center
of the custody battle that led Congressman Leo Ryan to investigate Jonestown, gave
me several hours of interviews. References to these unpublished interviews are given
by name and date.

who were involved in Peoples Temple but did not die at Jonestown. To "see" Layton and to "hear" the voice of her motivation and her love, one must deconstruct what one already knows about her—that she was a "cult" member, a woman sexually involved with a charismatic leader, and a suicide "victim."

3

The Triple Erasure of Women
in the Leadership of Peoples Temple

*T*he women of Peoples Temple, particularly the women in leadership, have been triply erased in the narratives about Jonestown,
whether scholarly or popular.[1] First, "cult" members as a whole, both
male and female, have been presented as "brainwashed" victims of a
fraudulent enterprise orchestrated by an "insane" leader. This has been
particularly the case in the popular literature on Jonestown, but a
perceptible thread of it runs throughout the scholarly material as well.
Second, within the treatments of new religions in Western culture as a
whole, wherever male charismatic leaders have predominated, female
followers have been portrayed as sexually exploited and psychologically manipulated at the hands of the cult leader. This characterization
is as true of the scholarly works as of the popular. Third, the fact that
the movement ended in suicide has erased the lives that preceded that
cataclysmic act, whether male or female.[2]

The erasure of the women of Peoples Temple has occurred because
the practice of the sociology of new religious movements has created
interpretive frameworks in which their experience simply has not fit.
As a result the data about their experience in Peoples Temple has
passed "beyond what could be conceptualized in the established forms,

---

1. I have put quotation marks around terms such as "cult," "brainwashed," "insane," and "normal" at first mention to indicate that these labels are ideologically
determined rather than scientifically established.

2. For the first and second examples of erasure, see this chapter and chapter 4. I
address the third example briefly at the close of this chapter, then reengage it in
chapter 7 where I explore a new interpretation of the suicides based on the restoration
of the people involved.

[therefore] we have learned to practice a discipline that disattends them or to find some way of making them over so that they will fit" (D. Smith 1987, 73). One must identify these interpretive schemata and the assumptions that are implicit in them regarding women in new religious movements.

Erasure through Membership in a "Cult"

The question as to whether people who join new religious movements have been brainwashed is a sociologically and politically over-determined one. The central institutions of mainstream Western society, such as the family, public schools, representative government, and mainstream religious organizations, are each invested in the proposition that "normal" persons can get their needs met within the legitimated structures of society.[3] This conviction is challenged when individuals join a new religious movement, particularly if they stay for an extended time and come from a white, educated, middle-class (or above) background. When this occurs, the ability of these institutions to meet the sociological, political, and psychological needs of their members is brought into question. Membership in a new religion specifically implies a critique of mainstream religious organizations but also of the consumer capitalist society that maintains and is maintained by them.[4] The potential cost to both the individual and the society is extremely high should the challenge be seen by others as legitimate. As Peter Berger points out:

> To go against the order of society is always to risk plunging into anomie. To go against the order of society as religiously legitimated, however, is to make a compact with the primeval forces of darkness. To deny reality as it has been socially defined is to risk falling into irreality, because it is well-nigh impossible in the long run to keep up alone and without social support one's own counter-definitions of the world. When the socially defined reality has come to be

3. I use the term *mainstream religious organizations* to refer to churches, synagogues, temples, and mosques where those organizations predominate within the mainstream of the social structure. Within the context of this study it refers primarily to the historical Protestant denominations, the Roman Catholic Church, and Reform Judaism.

4. For a sophisticated treatment of how religious institutions provide a "sacred canopy" for mainstream society, see Berger 1967, chap. 2.

identified with the ultimate reality of the universe, then its denial takes on the quality of evil as well as madness. The denier then risks moving into what may be called a negative reality—if one wishes, the reality of the devil. (Berger 1967, 39)

The ideological portrayal of the charismatic leader as insane and his followers as brainwashed is effective in maintaining the boundaries and values of mainstream society by delegitimating the challenge(s) of the new religion. As Bromley and Richardson point out, this function of the term *brainwashing* in maintaining the values of Western culture is embedded in the history from which it originated. Following Biderman (1962, 560), they note that *brainwashing* first came to be used as part of the anti-Communist rhetoric of the 1950s and 1960s where the assumption was that communist beliefs were "fundamentally alien to human nature and social reality" and that "the acceptance of Communist beliefs is consequently regarded as ipso facto evidence of insanity or a warped, evil personality, or both." Thus, brainwashing ideology is at its core anticommunitarian, antisocialist, and antitotalitarian. For this reason the shift in application of brainwashing from anti-Communist to anti–new religions was not a difficult one (Bromley and Richardson 1983, 6). Although the new religions that blossomed during the 1960s and 1970s in America were diverse in theology and practice, the challenges they presented to mainstream society tended to constellate in three areas. First, these groups generally accepted and acted upon a wider continuum of spiritual beliefs, practices, and experiences; obviously, a challenge to mainstream religious organizations. Second, most redefined family as religious community, a challenge to the nuclear family. Third, most viewed financial resources as belonging to the group rather than to the individual and tended to encourage the channeling of individual financial resources into the movement for group maintenance and mission, a challenge to consumer capitalism. Shupe and Bromley identify the challenges to family and economic order as particular areas of strain between the new religions and the families of members:

There were two major sources of strain between families and the new religions: a challenge, first, to the family's authority structure and second to its goal of preparing offspring for participation in the economic order. Families devoted much of their socialization activity to producing offspring capable of achieving socially and economically successful careers and lifestyles. (Shupe and Bromley 1981, 181)

In modern Western culture mainstream religious organizations have, for the most part, accommodated a split between private religious life and public secular life. The vast majority of Christian denominations in America have theologies and ministries that uphold the nuclear family and consumer capitalism, and offer few religious experiences that can claim authority over these mainstream institutions of secular life. Like most new religions, Peoples Temple challenged the gulf between private religiosity and public life by claiming the authority of the religious (Peoples Temple) over the public (American capitalist culture). Because religion is understood by the paradigms of scientific rationalism to be irrational and, for the most part, irrelevant in everyday life, the idea that a person would throw away success in mainstream society for membership in a new religion is seen as ludicrous. To do so unwillingly is brainwashing; to do so willingly is subversion. Freud's idea that religion is a kind of infantile wish fulfillment that one can grow out of is an idea that holds currency for the critics of new religions. He believed that what religious practitioners required to live as mature adults was an "education to reality" (Freud 1961, 63).

The "anticult movement," (Bromley and Shupe 1981) as scholars call the amalgam of groups who embrace the brainwashing theory,[5] cut its teeth in the legal battles against the Unification Church during the early 1970s. Dick Anthony, the most vociferous opponent of the brainwashing theory among the sociologists who study new religious movements, describes the theory's understanding of conversion:

> Converts have been "programmed" to claim adherence to an alien set of beliefs as the result of diabolically effective psychotechnological manipulation by the unscrupulous agents of the religious group. As the story goes, converts have no authentic interest in the groups they have joined and their true selves subsist in a kind of suspended animation while their bodies function essentially as robots controlled by their cultic masters. (Robbins and Anthony 1990, 295–96)

5. The Washington Council for American Family Foundation (AFF) and the Cult Awareness Network (CAN) are the most active and vocal on a national level in the United States.

Although this description might sound overdrawn as the statement of a critic, Margaret Singer, the leading proponent of the brainwashing theory, says:

> Charismatic, unscrupulous cult leaders such as David Koresh institute thought reform programs in order to ensure compliance among their followers. The belief systems of such groups are of secondary importance. . . . The belief systems' common characteristic is that they serve as "tools" to advance the leader's hidden agendas (which may sometimes be mere financial fraud, and other times, as with Koresh, the propping up of the leader's fragile and pathological ego). Members follow the leader not so much because of a rational and informed acceptance of the belief system, but because of the orchestrated program of psychological manipulation designed to gain their compliance. (Bardin, 1994, app. D)

Shupe and Bromley (1981, 186; 1980, 331) have summarized the major elements of this ideology as (1) cults are not legitimate religions but use religion as a "cloak" for "profit-making ventures operated by egomaniac charlatans for their own personal aggrandizement"; (2) people who join have not experienced a legitimate religious conversion but are "victims of deceptive, seductive, and/or manipulative processes that destroy their free will"; and (3) involvement in the cult is injurious to the member as an individual and dangerous for mainstream American social institutions, for example, the family, mainstream religious organizations, and democracy (Wilson 1981, 186; see also Shupe and Bromley 1980, 331). Anticult movement activists label the religious movement itself as wrong or evil and the members as brainwashed victims, which places all the power in the hands of the cult. The members of cults are seen by the anticult movement as both powerless and "innocent," thus they are in a condition to be restored to family and society.

Eileen Barker, in her study of people who have joined Unification Church, concluded that there are four variables at work when individuals "choose" to join a new religious movement: first, their hopes, fears, and values; second, their expectations of society; third, their general understanding of the attraction of the new religion; and fourth, the specific experiences of their interactions with the group (Barker 1984, 137). The choice to join a group is a result of a combination of these "pushes" and "pulls." Her participant observation of

Unification Church suggested to Barker that the group could only control the fourth variable (and that only to some extent) and influence the third but that it was not possible for Unification Church to "deceive" potential members into overriding their own personalities. As Barker has pointed out, the strongest proof against brainwashing is the high number of "non-joiners" who have some exposure to Unification Church when attending the two day, seven day, or twenty-one day workshops. As her data—and that of Galanter, (1983, 986)—demonstrate, the Unification Church recruitment process is at least "90 per cent *ineffective*" (147; italics in original).

Jonestown was, in many respects, a godsend for the anticult movement, for it demonstrated in graphic and horrifying terms what it had been warning parents and society against all along—that the kind of challenge to society that new religions represent does lead to "evil as well as madness" as Berger had suggested. "The ACM [anticult movement] used the Jonestown tragedy to promote its view of exotic religions. . . . In 1988, a major ACM drive promoted the tenth anniversary of the Jonestown tragedy with widely dispersed press packets stressing that cults brainwash members, and keep them through mind control practices" (Richardson, Best, and Bromley 1991, 8). Not only did Jonestown provide the anticult movement with its first martyr, Congressman Leo Ryan, and, more generally, in the more than two hundred children who died but it "objectified the anticultists' own worst fears about the destructive potential of cults and provided a concrete referent to which they could point as evidence in their appeals to the public and to political officials" (Levi 1982, 114).

The anticult movement's successful co-optation of Jonestown as a symbol of the danger of cults had the effect of utterly delegitimizing the challenges to mainstream society that Peoples Temple embodied. The Peoples Temple ministry to the disenfranchised in society was erased by the promotion of the view that Jim Jones only used concern for the poor, elderly, and blacks as a tool of manipulation in his fraudulent enterprise. Most of the books written just after the deaths at Jonestown were classic apostate stories with Jones depicted as evil or mad or both and his followers as brainwashed victims.[6]

Dorothy Smith has suggested that some theoretical constructs are so deeply embedded in the practice of a scholarly discipline that any

6. Among these books are Kerns and Wead 1979; Thielmann and Merrill 1979; Feinsod 1981; and, most notably, Mills 1979.

and all data seem to naturally "fit" into the categories that are presupposed. When disjunctures occur between the data and the theory, the datum, or "experienced actualities," as Smith calls these instances, are disregarded or recontextualized to fit the theory. Smith argues that sociology works within the parameters of an "ideological procedure." "The ideological circle as a method of producing an account selects from the primary narrative an array of particulars intending the ideological schema. The selection and assembly procedure discards competing reasons (*her* reasons) and permits the insertion of ideological connectives" (D. Smith 1990, 171; italics in original).

These ideological connectives span the informational distance between a "lived actuality" and the "interpretive schema" (D. Smith 1990, 152). To make sense out of a person's experience, certain assumptions come into play to fill the gap where either information or understanding fall short. Because the experience of people in new religions is so different from the experience of "normal" people in mainstream society, ideological connectives function for analysts of Jonestown in a particularly influential way. In fact, what Smith's theory suggests is that what one "knows" about Peoples Temple and about what happened at Jonestown on 18 November 1978 has more to do with the ideological schema being used by sociologists than with the lived experience of the people who were actually there. The task, then, if understanding and not merely persuasion is the goal, is to pull the account back into the sphere of influence of the lived actuality of the people who committed themselves to Peoples Temple and to allow their own words and behavior to challenge the authority of the interpretive schema. Still, even if a scholar is successful in doing this, Smith admits that although this method will "open up and expand how we know the world of our experience," it does not provide access to actual truth. What she is interested in identifying are the intellectual practices that cause people to discount information that could be important in evaluating the power dynamic in social relations (1990, 200–201). She does not value experience more than analysis but sees a person's lived actuality as a necessary starting point if one's understanding is not to be censored by one's analytical schema (D. Smith 1987, 89).

Certainly, the madman-brainwashed victim scenario is one such instance of an interpretive schema that is so laden with assumptions that any evidence running contrary to it is filtered out by the analyst. Examples of sanity on the part of the leader and agency on the part of the followers are either discounted or made further examples of the diabolical nature of the movement. ("Look, the cult leader can even make his followers *appear* normal!") This interpretive schema has dominated the analysis of Jonestown to such an extent that otherwise careful journals, such as *Political Psychology*, have published articles on Jonestown that include such unsubstantiated conclusions as: "The charismatic leader weaves a hypnotic spell over the members of a mass movement. Under such a 'mass hypnosis,' the members of a mass movement may blindly follow the orders of a charismatic leader as in a day dream or trance" (Ulman and Abse 1983, 641).

The media have played a central role in reflecting and constructing this view of cults for popular consumption. In "The Social Construction and Interpretation of Deviance: Jonestown and the Mass Media" (1980) Danny Jorgensen argues that the role of the media in constructing as well as reflecting reality is especially apparent in its coverage of cults. Partly, this complicity exists because apostates with an atrocity story to tell make themselves readily available to reporters; partly, because new religious movements have learned to be suspicious of the media and, therefore have not been open to investigative reporters writing stories on their movement from an insider's perspective. Besides a lack of information about the actual lived experience of people within new religious movements, the media is attracted to sensational stories. As mentioned in chapter 2, most atrocity stories feature accusations of food and sleep deprivation, sexual and physical abuse, and excesses of spiritual and emotional authority by the charismatic leader. Fear about the safety of children within cults has begun to play a more central role in the anticult movement accusations about the activities of new religions. The allegation of child abuse within the Branch Davidian compound at Waco, Texas, was the accusation that drove the decision to use tanks and gas to end the siege on 19 April 1993. This attempt to "save the children" resulted in the deaths of all the children in residence at the compound, and the allegations of child abuse were later proven to have been groundless. These are subjects for which the public has shown a voracious appetite. Less commented upon is the implicit assumption by journalists that none of their audience could possibly be involved in such a group. Cult leaders and members are treated as completely "other" than the audience. This was especially true in the case of the media coverage of Jonestown, which was widespread and consistent in its portrayal of the madman-brainwashed victim schema.

In every sense Jonestown was a big story. One month after the tragedy a Gallup Poll showed that 98 percent of the American public had heard about Peoples Temple and the Jonestown suicides. Only Pearl Harbor and the dropping of the atomic bombs in Japan had equaled this level of public awareness (Barker 1986, 330). *Christianity Today* reported in 1979 that "the major secular media in the United States gave more coverage to the People's Temple tragedy than to any other single religion-related story in recent memory. That includes the election and death of Pope John Paul I and the subsequent election of John Paul II" (Jorgensen 1980, 314). In part this was the case because the Jonestown incident occurred during a traditionally slow news period, the week before the American Thanksgiving. That the event was "bizarre" and tragic also contributed to its popularity as a news subject.

Commentators have also observed that the media took the Jonestown tragedy very personally because some of their own—NBC correspondent Don Harris, NBC cameraman Bob Brown, and *San Francisco Examiner* photographer Greg Robinson—were murdered by Peoples Temple members at the Port Kaituma airstrip. This involvement may have contributed to the amount of coverage given and certainly to its content in that Don Harris, particularly, was presented within the motif "journalist as hero."[7]

Danny Jorgensen, who surveyed all the coverage of Jonestown in the United States from 19 November through 26 November 1978, notes that explanations of Jonestown emerged within days of the event and that these explanations were repeated so often that they began to carry "symbolic significance." "This explanation involved three important components: The People's Temple was labeled a *cult*, Jones was held to be *depraved*, and the members of the group were defined as *deprived*" (Jorgensen 1980, 317; italics in original). Most coverage included all three components, generally with an exploration of the "socioeconomic deprivation or psychological abnormality" of the members, which left them open to the abuses of Jones's insanity, and the combination of which created the Peoples Temple cult (Jorgensen 1980, 321–22). Together they created a tightly woven ideological fabric nearly impossible to penetrate with other perspectives. As Jorgensen discovered when following the experience of scholars whose views were solicited by reporters but not used: "notions at odds with

7. See Nimmo and Combs 1985, chap. 1.

common sense are unlikely to be reported or even to be recognized as explanations from the news perspective" (322–23). Common sense for the news media who cover new religious movements is generally determined by what they have heard about the movement from former members. As Shupe and Bromley point out:

> Virtually all of the public "knowledge" about the new religions . . . has been obtained indirectly from accounts in the media, a substantial proportion of which was initiated by opponents of the new religions in general and apostates in particular. Because these individuals have often been readily accorded credibility by the media, they have had a disproportionate influence in setting the agenda for public discussion of the new religions. (Wilson 1981, 181).

The use of the term *cult* in reference to Peoples Temple, with all that it implies about the emotional or social instability of its members (dramatically confirmed by the death they chose), created an impassable distance between the American public and those who died at Jonestown. In an angry denunciation of the way the bodies of her sisters, Carolyn Layton and Ann Moore, and the other Peoples Temple deceased had been treated, Rebecca Moore demonstrates how the full humanity of the cultists was called into question:

> If you're a cultist, you don't have the same civil rights ordinary Americans enjoy. If you die, the government doesn't have to perform an autopsy, or investigate your death. It can entertain the notion of dumping you into a mass grave. It can destroy evidence of the cause of your death, frustrate your family's efforts to secure your remains, stick you in an airport hangar on a military base 3,000 miles from home for weeks on end, and depend upon public apathy to get away with it. (Moore 1988, 91)

It was not "public apathy" alone that allowed the United States government to "get away with it" but the dehumanizing power of an ideological schema that caused the Jonestown dead to appear totally "other" than the mainstream population.[8] This erasure of its members is especially ironic because Peoples Temple was more representative in its membership—in race, age, and class—than any other new religious movement that has been studied. Demographically, Peoples Temple

---

8. For more on this schema, see Chidester 1988, 681–702.

was "us." Yet the label *cult* made Peoples Temple "them." The people who died at Jonestown were truly "the most intimate other."

Erasure Through Sex with the Leader

A less-visible yet equally powerful interpretive schema in the study of new religious movements is that of the sexual exploitation of the female follower by the male charismatic leader. Here, assumptions about men and women are embedded in the schema applied to new religions. Even in the case of Peoples Temple, in which there is clear evidence of women exercising institutional authority, their power is addressed in the scholarly literature almost always in the context of the women's sexual relationship with Jim Jones.

What is the interpretive schema that frames what has been written about women involved in new religious movements and their relationship to the male charismatic leader? First, there is the primacy of sexual pleasure as a "legitimate" motivation for the male charismatic leader to become sexually involved with his followers. In fact, no other motivation need be demonstrated by the scholar. It is assumed that if a male leader could have sex with his followers, he naturally would for the enjoyment it would afford him. To deconstruct the gendered assumptions that undergird this point, all one needs to do is look at its opposite case. If a female follower claims that she wants to have sex with the leader for pleasure, this is raised as additional evidence that she has been brainwashed (an anticult movement argument) or victimized (mainstream new religious movement scholars). The assumption undergirding these conclusions is that only an "aberrant" or maladjusted woman would want sex for the sake of sex but that men (especially men in power) "normally" want sex and the pleasure it affords. (This is an expression of a wide-spread cross-cultural belief that sex is dirty and that a woman who enjoys sex is a "slut.") There are issues of power here, of course, which are addressed in chapter 4, but the point raised at present is that sexual activity is seen as a legitimate, normal desire for a male charismatic leader but not a motive for a female follower unless something is wrong with her.

The second component of this "sex in cults" interpretive schema is that in addition to sexual pleasure the charismatic leader may have sex with his followers for a utilitarian reason. Sex may be used as a way to gain deeper loyalty from individual members or, if he has sex with more than one follower, a way to keep the women competitive with one another by using a "divide and conquer" strategy. This interpretation assumes that the leader is interested in keeping power (part of the normative anticult movement interpretive schema), not in building a community. It also fails to take into account the possibility of sex between a female follower and male leader as being utilitarian for the woman *and* the man; or, if this is taken into consideration, the relationship is depicted as a "secretary sleeping with the boss" scenario in which the woman is portrayed as a manipulative seductress.

Third is the assumption that all the power is in the hands of the charismatic leader and that other than sexual pleasure or political manipulation, the leader has nothing to gain from contact with the specific woman follower with whom he has sex. Deeply entrenched cultural assumptions regarding women and the nature of sexuality are embedded in this belief in the charismatic leader as all powerful: (1) that women are easily manipulated sexually; (2) that, once sexual relations are introduced into a male-female relationship, the woman's power, insight, and abilities disappear; (3) that sex (and occasionally issues concerning domesticity) are definitive of women involved in new religious movements; and (4) that sex is primarily about male-female coitus with sexuality rarely addressed as a larger, more diffuse dynamic in the group.

The work of Andres Pavlos on women in new religions is typical of a perspective that blends the brainwashing and "sex in cults" schemata:

> On the verbal level, some religious leaders promulgate feminism; however in reality, the low valuation of women in cults is often expressed most directly in a common cult practice that demands that males be eagerly served as avatars by the cult's females. Most females are only tolerated as economic resources as they serve to advance the patriarchal lineage of the cult leader. (Pavlos 1982, 132–33)

This book typifies the anticult movement tendency to treat all cults as the same no matter what their theological, sociological, or philosophical diversity.

Because of the proclivity for male charismatic leaders and even male members to take sexual, economic, and emotional advantage of female members, a situation that is endemic to cults according to Pavlos, a woman's status is never improved by joining a new religious movement. He concludes that the greater opportunities afforded women in the secular world, as a result of the successes of the feminist movement, mean that women will leave cults in greater numbers than ever.[9]

To hear the voices of the women of Jonestown one must deconstruct this gendered understanding of power and sexuality in new religions. I do so by examining how a woman in the leadership of Peoples Temple, Carolyn Moore Layton, has been portrayed in the secondary literature, with an emphasis on the best of the scholarly treatments. In chapter 4, I introduce evidence about her power and influence and that of a number of other women in the leadership of Peoples Temple. In other studies this information has been filtered out through the "sex in cults" interpretive framework.

The best of the secondary literature on Peoples Temple is John Hall's (1987) study. One of the puzzling aspects of the history of Peoples Temple that he attempts to explain is how a small group of religious devotees from Indiana, numbering no more than seventy when they migrated to California during the summer of 1965, could grow into a major political and religious movement numbering more than three thousand members by the early 1970s (see chap. 5). His answer was that a fundamental shift occurred in the organization when white, educated professionals began joining Peoples Temple. He mentions by name Linda Amos, Larry and Carolyn Layton, Elmer and Deanna Mertle, and Timothy Oliver Stoen, asserting that the involvement of these people with their "organizational skills and social prominence . . . helped propel the group toward an entirely different scale of operations" (66). What is interesting from the perspective of an analysis of gender is where Hall proceeds after establishing this general point. He writes two paragraphs, one each about Carolyn Layton and Timothy Stoen, respectively, in which he asserts that Layton's contribution to Peoples Temple was to cause a "social transformation [which] stemmed from a relationship that developed between Jim Jones and newcomer Carolyn Layton" while Stoen "marshalled his considerable organizational talents and professional

9. The pro-feminist note in Pavlos's work, "as a feminist you must be naturally opposed to the subjugation and abuse of women which takes place in cults," has arisen in many of the informal conversations I have had with anticult movement activists. For more on the relationship between feminism and anticult activism, see Richardson, Best, and Bromley 1991, chap. 5.

connections to help Jones build a powerful social movement" (66). Stoen's contributions along this vein are irrefutable; however, he was not alone in establishing Peoples Temple as the influential religious and political organization that it became during the 1970s. Carolyn Layton was as much at the center of building and maintaining the organization of Peoples Temple and later, Jonestown, as was Tim Stoen, perhaps even more so (see chap. 4). The fact, however, that she was Jones's long-term sexual partner and mother of one of his children has caused scholars to discount or marginalize this evidence in conformity with the ideological schema reviewed above.

It would be well to remember at this point that Dorothy Smith makes clear that a sociologist does not have to be a sexist to practice a scholarly discipline that is constituted from certain gendered assumptions. I am not, therefore, arguing that Hall or any of the writers on Peoples Temple whom I critique are sexist but that the schemata they use *presuppose* a certain kind of relationship between the charismatic leader and women in new religions, which Hall, Weightman (1983), and others have applied noncritically.

Within a well-researched piece such as Hall's there are bound to be tensions between data and interpretive schema. (Ideologically based schemata hold up best where the least amount of research is done.) This is certainly the case in his portrayal of Carolyn Layton. Sometimes this tension is embodied in a single sentence. For example, when writing about the administrative capabilities of Layton from the perspective of a highly placed Temple member, Hall begins the sentence with "[Jones's] lover and closest companion, Carolyn Layton," thus firmly placing her in the sexual-domestic sphere, but then completes the sentence with Teri Buford describing Layton as "the top of the line" within the Peoples Temple organization. Because this causes a clear interpretive discontinuity within the schema traditionally used, Hall must resolve the conflict and decide whether Layton is, in fact, a sexual partner or an organizational leader. He does so two sentences later. The entire section is quoted below so excerpted portions can be read in context.

Paralleling Weber's description of the charismatic community in general, one member of Jones's staff would be in charge of security; another, counseling; yet another would oversee the Needs Department, and so forth. . . . Jones used his personal secretaries as envoys to the wider network. His lover and closest companion, Carolyn

Layton, probably was "the top of the line," as Teri Buford later put it. Buford herself worked for years as the liaison between Jones, various departments, and Tim Stoen (for whom she also worked directly). But based on his legal training, Stoen had greater organizational expertise than Carolyn Layton or Teri Buford, and according to various Temple members, including Jones himself, Stoen probably knew more about the operations of Peoples Temple than any single person aside from Jones. (Hall 1987, 99)

Buford's comment about Layton being "the top of the line" is used by Hall in the context of his having described her as one of Jones's "personal secretaries." This is a slippery designation at best, in that Layton was involved in organizational strategies for the Temple and, from her training as a high school government teacher, was more interested in theorizing about the movement as a utopian community than in the kinds of tasks commonly associated with secretarial work. Even in their leadership roles, the women of Peoples Temple are segregated into the specifically gendered role of secretary. A more appropriate designation for the kind of work performed by Carolyn Layton, and by Maria Katsaris and Teri Buford would certainly have been administrators or executive officers. By referring to Layton as a secretary and then as "lover and companion" to Jones, Hall alludes to the ideological schema of the secretary having sex with the boss in order to move up in the organization. By contextualizing Layton's organizational authority in this way Hall makes it difficult to believe that she could have been both Jones' sexual partner *and* "the top of the line," an argument that I make in chapter 4.

Hall goes to great length to outline the variety of social services offered by Peoples Temple to members and the financial sophistication required to do so. Carolyn Layton is mentioned as involved in many of these enterprises, including providing counseling after worship services (along with Tim Stoen) "about everything from automobile accidents to welfare eligibility" (Hall 1987, 82); depositing money in numerous bank accounts (89); and being designated as the named recipient (often together with Stoen) of wills or "life-care" agreements (93). Nonetheless, he describes her in terms that would be unthinkable if he were writing about a male in the group and that are based on little more than the ideological schema within which he is working. "For her part, Carolyn *passed time* in the early California years *playing* with the Jones children; she *sought to nurture a friendship* with Marcie and *fretted* over Karen Layton, the young woman who had married her former husband Larry, for 'the countless times she has looked flirtatiously at Jim' (126; italics added).

It is not the factual basis of this sentence I dispute but the way in which it contextualizes Carolyn Layton's work in Peoples Temple as being about her relationship with Jim Jones and not (equally) about her commitment to Peoples Temple as a movement, which represented the very challenges to society (outlined earlier in this chapter) to which she was most committed.

Judith Weightman (1983) concentrates more specifically on the women of Peoples Temple than does Hall. Her understanding of the women in leadership places them even more firmly within the confines of the "sex in cults" interpretive framework than does Hall's. There is no question that Jones had sexual relations with many, if not most, of the women in leadership. His long-term relationship with his wife and Carolyn Layton did not preclude his being involved sexually with others. Weightman argues that Jones's widespread and nonexclusive sexual activity is one of the psychological tools he used to manipulate and control his leadership circle. She points out that by November 1978 nearly all the members of the inner circle were women who became part of the elite "not only because of their abilities but also because of their loyalty to the cause and their intense personal loyalty to Jones. For the most part, this personal loyalty was very much connected with the fact that they were, or had been, Jones's lovers (117). This question of loyalty will become a central issue when the dynamics behind the decision to commit suicide are explored in chapters 6 and 7.[10]

Weightman quotes widely from the books of people who had left Peoples Temple or had lost loved ones there. She is noncritical in her use of these materials and conveys the information contained in them as though they were factual reports of the events, even going so far as to suggest that there are two possible exceptions to her critique of brainwashing as a reason for people having been involved in Peoples Temple: one of the exceptions was Maria Katsaris, the daughter of her central informant, the other, Larry Layton, who she thinks may have

---

10. It is important to note that most of the speculation about the Jonestown suicides has focused on why the members of Peoples Temple were willing to commit suicide once they were told to do so. My analysis is more concerned with why and how the decision was made in the first place.

been "brainwashed" because he "had two wives co-opted by Jones" (Weightman 1983, 160, 164). She uses the experience of Deborah Layton Blakey, who had several sexual encounters with Jones before defecting in May 1978, and who felt that Jones' preference for her had made her a rival to Carolyn Layton and Maria Katsaris, to make the broad point that "the female members of the elite were divided by sexual jealousy, division encouraged by Jones, who urged them to keep tabs on each other" (118). Because her evidence for this sexual jealousy is so scant, it is difficult to weigh its credibility, but my conclusion is that it is an assumption built into the framework of her analysis.

In the paragraph after her treatment of rivalry among the females in the inner circle she writes about the male elite. What is notable in this paragraph is how the names of the men are each preceded by the title of his official function in the organization, whereas the list of women two pages earlier had described all of them as "young, attractive, white women" (Weightman 1983, 117). It is worth noting, too, that she does not speculate about the emotional motivation for the men's loyalty either to Jones or the movement, nor does she explore their relationship with one another as she had with the women.

> There were some male members of the elite as well. Assistant Pastor Jack Beam, Temple attorneys Eugene Chaikin and Tim Stoen, and Temple public relations person Michael Prokes were most significant among them. . . . Although the women members of the elite were "initiated" through sexual encounters with Jones, there is no evidence as to whether or not these men had sex with Jones. Stoen and [Larry] Layton both publicly "confessed" their homosexuality, though without mentioning Jones by name. For both of these men, however, an actual sexual encounter would be unnecessary, because Jones had achieved effectively the same end by co-opting their wives. (119).

The men are presented to the reader within a framework different from that of the women. Jones's relationships with Stoen and Larry Layton are mediated through his sexual relationship with their wives, according to Weightman. The schema she uses is, ironically, a reflection of the behavior that she criticizes in Jones: women are not individuals in their own right but are extensions of the men with whom they are sexually involved. Carolyn Layton is introduced in this chapter as Larry Layton's wife and as one of Jim Jones's "most important mistresses" (Weightman 1983, 138). In the introduction to her book in a list of people associated with the Peoples Temple, Carolyn Moore Layton is described as "Larry's first wife, she became, with Maria Katsaris, one of Jones's two most important mistresses." Weightman's assumption is that the sex between Jones and the women was all a power play between him and the husbands of these women. Jones had sex with his female followers to humiliate the men and to manipulate the women. There is no space within Weightman's thesis to entertain the possibility that the women may have been having sex with Jones in an attempt to exercise power within the community. Within her framework only Jones can "initiate" relationships and only the men act. An interesting example of factual inaccuracy in support of this gender-biased schema are the two lines following the paragraph quoted above: "Larry was the first member of the Layton family to join the Temple. He brought with him his wife, Carolyn Moore Layton, with whom Jones became enamored" (119). The men have all the agency in this passage with Larry "joining" and Jones becoming "enamored," whereas Carolyn is either an appendage or object of the men's behavior. In fact, all the accounts of Carolyn and Larry Layton's initial involvement in Peoples Temple suggest that either it was a joint decision or that Carolyn had initiated it.

Weightman underscores the importance of sex in the Peoples Temple leadership structure. She argues that "Jones created the elite of the Temple by making them his property, or by taking the property of his male followers. He marked out his property by having sex with selected individuals" (Weightman 1983, 120). Using the work of Susan Brownmiller (1975) on rape, Weightman maintains that Jones's sexual relationship with the women was aggrandizing for him and dehumanizing for them. Yet, while persisting with the property metaphor, she concedes a point that is the subject of chapter 4—that having sex with Jones gave the women power. Weightman writes that "a sexual relationship with Jones . . . may have appealed to the women because it gave them access to power, power unobtainable in any other way" (121). The power she is referring to is access to the financial dealings of the Temple and the "research" for the bogus healing practices of the early California years. I argue, however, that the power these women, particularly Carolyn Moore Layton, possessed was not derivative, but central. It was the power to influence Jim Jones and the authority to make decisions about the day-to-day functioning of Peoples Temple.

Weightman's thesis is an ideal example of the "sex in cults" perspective. The main components of this schema—(1) sexual pleasure is a "legitimate" motive for a charismatic leader to have sex with his female followers, but not vice versa; (2) sex is often used in a utilitarian way to "divide and conquer" female followers; and (3) power flows from the leader to the followers and, other than pleasure or control, the leader has nothing to gain from his female followers—contextualize a woman's commitment to the new religion she has joined and any power or authority she might exercise within her sexual relationship with the leader. Thus, for women, sex precludes power. She is an object of desire and manipulation without sexual or psychological agency of her own. (Whether this theory might apply to heterosexual relationships outside of new religions is a question beyond the purview of this study.) In my view, this is a sophisticated extension of the brainwashing theory, one which is gender specific. It suggests that once a woman has had sex with a leader she can no longer think for herself or control her behavior.

A different framework for understanding sex and power within new religious movements provides a new perspective on why Jonestown ended in the way that it did. By restoring the power and agency of Carolyn Layton and other female leaders within Peoples Temple one gains a new understanding of what happened during its final months. A starting point for this inquiry is to ask what the possible benefits would be to a woman follower in a sexual relationship with a male charismatic leader.

First, she may become a person with "favored status" within the religious community. Because the authority of a new religious movement is most frequently embodied in the charismatic leader, the closer a follower is to the leader, the more deflected authority the individual obtains. In addition, people within the organization know that the woman who is having sex with the leader can act as a conduit for information both from the leader to the community and from the community back to the leader. Thus, a woman in a sexual relationship with the charismatic leader functions as both "gatekeeper," filtering and distilling important information about the community for the leader's consumption, and "communications officer," transmitting information from the leader in an informal way back into the community. Another possible benefit for a woman who sleeps with the charismatic leader is that she has more casual time with the leader than other members of the movement do. In addition, "pillow talk" may serve as an important time for the woman follower to educate the leader about the movement. It is a time when great influence can be exercised and much teaching and learning can take place that does not necessarily flow exclusively from the "leader" to the "follower." Within charismatically organized groups the leader tends to become conflated in the mind of the follower with the movement itself. It is possible that a woman who loves and nurtures the charismatic leader may, in fact, be serving the community and the cause embodied in the person of the leader.

Far from the assumption in the "sex in cults" interpretive framework, that a woman's power is invalidated through her sexual relationship with the leader, this new framework suggests that she gains more authority and influence within the community of which she is a member by having a sexual relationship with the charismatic leader. The major methodological difference between these two schemata is that the routinely used framework ("sex in cults") derives from an "outsider" perspective, whereas the approach here ("sex and power") draws upon the experience of people on the inside. Smith points out that a sociologist's evaluation of the dynamics at work in an organization shifts when the words of actual participants, particularly women, are taken seriously and are allowed to challenge the theoretical schema being employed. "A sociology for women preserves the presence of subjects as knowers and as actors. It does not transform subjects into objects of study or make use of conceptual devices for eliminating the active presence of subjects. Its methods of thinking and its analytic procedures must preserve the presence of the active and experiencing subject" (D. Smith 1987, 105).

Although she calls this a "sociology for women" her interests are broader than carving out a niche for women's roles to be explored within the traditional paradigms of sociology. Rather, she is interested in a radical shift in the way sociology is practiced. Her method requires that sociological inquiry begin with those (insider) experiences of everyday life that challenge the theoretical abstractions that control the scholar's (outsider) understanding of social forms and behavior. Smith's critique of the way in which ideological schemata control what sociologists identify as data extends to the third way in which the women of Peoples Temple have been erased in the narratives— the obliterating power of suicide.

Erasure Through Suicide

Dorothy Smith has argued that the designation "suicide" serves to focus and contain the experience of the person's death in such a way that it makes "the act of self killing" more comprehensible to those left behind (D. Smith 1990, 142). At the same time, it limits "relevant" information about the actions and events that, apparently, led to the person's suicide. She uses as her case the death of Virginia Woolf and suggests other ways of interpreting her act of "self killing" aside from the diagnosis of Woolf as mentally ill. Smith argues that Bell's biography of Woolf is little more than a narrative about a woman's mental illness that culminated in suicide. Thus, those who commit "suicide" have relinquished their right to a biography that takes in the fullness and variety of the life they led (D. Smith 1990, chap. 7). Those who lost loved ones at Jonestown have expressed a similar kind of frustration over the way in which the Peoples Temple ministry and the lives of those who contributed to it have been subsumed within the "mass suicide." It is as though suicide has the power to erase the life that led to it.

Along with the writer of a suicide account, the reader plays an interpretive role when the word *suicide* is used. The ideological connective that the reader provides is the belief that only mentally ill or emotionally unbalanced people kill themselves. Therefore, everything that Woolf did in the months before her suicide was understood by the psychiatric specialists, her husband, and the reader of the narratives about her life as evidence of her mental illness. "Acts, utterances, and expressed feelings are reconstructed as constituents of a course of illness or a psychic syndrome" (D. Smith 1990, 194). This belief about the link between mental illness and suicide has contributed to the erasure of the members of Peoples Temple. As Smith points out, Woolf's "subjectivity" is "subdued" by a schema that assumes that suicide is *never* a rational choice. More to the point, this interpretive strategy has made it difficult, if not impossible, to consider seriously the motives of those who planned the suicide at Jonestown.

Yet the irrationality of suicide was not always assumed. William Willimon comments on the tendency for the interpretations of what happened at Jonestown to focus on either the insane leader–brainwashed followers explanation or the psychosocial deprivation theory. He writes, "Both theories assumed that in the modern world only insane people would die for what they believed." By contrast, early

Christian history is rife with accounts of people "who quite joyfully parted with possessions, family, friends, even life itself in order to remain faithful" (Willimon 1988, 66). In modern America "freedom of religion" does not include the freedom to care so deeply and so strongly about religion as to include losing one's life for it. "We are free to exercise our faith—as long as we do so within certain limits, as long as I do not become a fanatic—like the poor, deranged folk at Jonestown who committed suicide rather than forsake their belief in Jim Jones. Although we have freedom to be religious, that does not seem to involve freedom to die for what we believe, because only a crazed fanatic would do that" (Willimon 1988, 66).

I suggest that it was not belief in Jim Jones as much as belief in Jonestown that the leaders of Peoples Temple were not willing to forsake. Nonetheless, Willimon's larger point is well taken. Deeply held religious commitments are simply not the norm in modern Western culture. So the final act of the people of Jonestown not only appears irrational but decidedly archaic. No wonder the schemata of brainwashing and deprivation hold so much currency: religious commitment itself, not to mention the commitment to justice that was at the center of the Peoples Temple theology-philosophy, is not what is valued in the Western world today. It is far easier to think of Jonestown entirely in terms of the suicides and to allow that interpretive schema to erase the ideals of Peoples Temple than to embrace the challenges of their ministry and to look at how deeply the people engaged in it cared. To do so would make the members of Peoples Temple martyrs and would legitimate the choice they made, even glorify it.

Umberto Eco points out that martyrdom is an old theme in Western religious history. Commenting on the bloody history of Christianity and the relationship of the Peoples Temple suicides to it, he writes:

Suicide is not the rule in all these movements, but violent death—bloodbath, destruction on the pyre—certainly is. And it is easy to understand why the theme of suicide . . . seems to become popular only today; the reason is that for those past movements the desire for martyrdom, death, and purification was satisfied by the authorities in power. . . . [When] authority refuses to administer death, the desire for martyrdom must take on more active forms: *Do it yourself*, in short. (Eco 1979, 99; italics in original)

The decision to commit suicide makes sense in the context of a history of martyrdom that is largely ignored in modern Western culture. So, it is not only the members of Peoples Temple who have been erased but the history of religious commitment with the sacrifical choices believers sometimes make in defense of their community and beliefs.

4

A Restoration of Women's Power
in Peoples Temple

*T*he women and men in the leadership of Peoples Temple shared
one thing in common: all had a strong desire to contribute posi-
tively and centrally to social change. Steve Rose, theologian and early
analyst of Jonestown, named this desire the "Herculean conscience,"
which is

> an overwhelming desire to do good. . . . [It] defines the attitude of a
> small portion of the American populace, a group of people whose
> consciousness is formed by an existential awareness of major destruc-
> tive forces in the world and by a strong desire to do something to
> combat them. The concerns of such individuals go far beyond the
> narrow pockets of self-interest to war and peace, ecological balance,
> social justice, and human rights. (Rose 1979, 22)

I suggest that there is a difference between how this desire
manifested itself in the women and the men in positions of authority in Peoples Temple. For the women, it wasn't until they met Jim
Jones and joined Peoples Temple that their personal power and institutional influence matched their desire to make a difference in the
world. For the men, it would have been possible eventually to act out
this desire in positions of leadership in mainstream society. For the
women, this would have been less likely because of the "glass ceiling"
within mainstream society that limits the authority women can exercise. Within Peoples Temple there was an opportunity for some
women to exercise power and authority beyond what either their

gender or educational training would have allowed in mainstream society.[1]

When reflecting on her personality and character, the people who knew her best described Carolyn Moore Layton as somebody who "had to be involved in changing the world" (Moore 1985, 85). The child of a United Methodist minister and a woman who was devoted to caring for social outcasts, Layton was raised with a commitment to social change and a prophetic interpretation of Christ's presence in the world. Her sister, Rebecca Moore, who did not join the Temple, although her sisters Carolyn and Annie encouraged her to do so, saw the seeds of her sister's commitment to Peoples Temple in the liberal Protestant upbringing they had experienced in their family.

> Ironically, it was our own religious training that made Carolyn an activist and prepared her for Peoples Temple. The message of the Bible was clear: serve the poor. But the churches she'd known didn't seem to care about the poor, at least, not enough. The pietism of traditional white Protestantism bored and frustrated her. What did evangelism and prayer have to do with feeding hungry people or caring for the sick? (85)

Layton was highly intelligent with interests in the social sciences, politics, and international affairs. Her family described her as "outgoing, aggressive, ambitious" although this exterior "disguised a basic lack of self-confidence" (Moore 1985, 87). She married Larry Layton in 1967 and began teaching high school in the town neighboring Redwood Valley, where Peoples Temple relocated from Indiana, in 1965. Peoples Temple offered Carolyn Layton a church community committed to the social justice and outreach ministries that most interested her: care for the poor, elderly, and mentally ill; commitment to racial integration; willingness to critique and to challenge unjust and unfair governmental policies.

Shortly after becoming involved in Peoples Temple, Carolyn Layton and Jim Jones began a sexual relationship that culminated in their having a child together, Jim-Jon, in 1975. It was a deeply satisfying

---

1. Rose argues that there is a dangerous flip-side to the Herculean conscience, which Jim Jones embodied, "the Herculean paranoid style" (Rose 1979, 24]). This became the style of many of the women in leadership once the move to Jonestown had been made.

love affair for Layton as she intimated in a letter to her sister Rebecca in 1970:

> Our communication is so deep that we can often know the other's emotions. I naturally have no parapsychological power and am very down-to-earth, but I know him so well I often can tell how he will feel about things. He knows more about me than I know myself and always accepts me totally. Total acceptance and communication make our love deeper than I thought possible between two humans. (Moore 1985, 90)

Layton's ability to know how Jones would "feel about things" would become increasingly crucial as drugs and paranoia crippled his ability to manage Peoples Temple once the group had moved to Jonestown.

Carolyn Moore Layton was at the center of the Peoples Temple decision-making apparatus from early in her membership until the very end. At the 8 October 1973 Board of Directors meeting for Peoples Temple, the meeting at which it was decided to establish "an agricultural mission in the tropics" in Guyana, South America, Layton was authorized, along with five others, to withdraw monies for the purchase of equipment, material, and supplies for the mission. (The other five members were Jim Jones, Archie Ijames, Timothy Stoen, Eugene Chaikin, and Marceline Jones.[2]

Throughout 1974 Layton and Timothy Oliver Stoen traded off chairing the monthly meetings until both their terms as directors on the board expired in January 1975. During Layton's time on the board Guyana was set up as a mission project and the first visit to the project by a group of Peoples Temple members were made. This was also the beginning of the time when the leaders of Peoples Temple began to consider the mission in Guyana as a possible retreat from the "hostile and offensive" behavior the community had experienced from residents of Redwood Valley, particularly toward the black members. The 9 September 1974 minutes note that "a number of the members of the Board speculated that if this type of harassment continued, it might be necessary, at some future date, for all the members of the church, for their own protection, to move out of Mendocino area into some other facility."[3] In a résumé written in 1976, Layton described herself

2. Federal Bureau of Investigation (FBI), Guyana Evidence Index, 89-4286.
3. FBI, Guyana Evidence Index, 89-4286.

as the "Vice President and Director of the Peoples Temple of the Disciples of Christ, with over 40,000 members in California and outreach missionary programs in many other states and abroad." And "I was directly assisting the Pastor and President of this church and was involved in helping to structure this large and successful group from its inception in California, with around 75 initial members, to its present growth and size."

She indicated that her responsibilities included

> budget planning and follow-up administration; selection and final approval of Advisory Personnel; opening of new branches, training staff and members to staff and operate branches; travel abroad and dealing with foreign governmental dignitaries on behalf of the church's foreign missionary programs; Advisory Chairman of church's financial investments, researching projects and reporting to its President and Pastor, and sharing of administration of the Board of Directors, in its regular and special functions; and Assistant to the President and Pastor. (CHS, L-2, L-5)

It is difficult to determine how much of an influence Carolyn Layton had on the specific decisions that were made by Jim Jones and the inner circle of Peoples Temple. She was, after all, a leader within a self-consciously socialist community, in which heavy-handed or individually aggrandizing authority was not acceptable behavior by anyone except Jim Jones. Jones was given a kind of special dispensation in this regard because of his status as prophet and founder. Her role and influence must be pieced together through reading between the lines of the narrative deconstructed in chapter 3 and through reconstructing her possible influence and authority.

In letters to her parents written from Jonestown Layton indicates that her primary responsibilities at Jonestown were educational and organizational. She had moved to Guyana in the spring of 1977, several months before Jones arrived and the major relocation of people was complete. By the fall of 1977 she was concentrating most of her attention on the Jonestown school system. "I am teaching political science in our high school. I do a lot of teaching of political philosophy which I have always wanted to do as you may recall. This is the first time I have ever been able to teach what I really have wanted. Also I help administrate the high school and train younger teachers" (Moore 1986, 190).

Layton was well qualified for this work, having graduated from the University of California with a Bachelor of Arts degree in political science and a teaching credential. Before moving to Jonestown she had been a high school teacher in the Ukiah Unified School District for seven years. The subjects she taught were government, history, economics, geography, French, and physical education. Her letters are filled with information about the agricultural production of the settlement and the planning for eventual self-sufficiency as a community. As she wrote to her parents in November 1977, "we do a lot of planning-production goals, etc. Obviously the more planning we do, the better productivity we get on the farm. As you know, I have always wanted to teach these subjects and this is the first time I have ever been able to teach what I really wanted to teach. So I am really enjoying this" (Moore 1986, 198).

After the suicides, the FBI was concerned that surviving members of the Peoples Temple were organizing a "hit squad" to kill the people who they thought had been involved in a conspiracy to end the movement. Many of the people the FBI interviewed, most of whom were members who had left the group before the move to Jonestown, mentioned Carolyn Layton as an important person for the FBI to be aware of in its search for potential leaders who might be continuing the post-Jonestown work of Peoples Temple.[4] At the time of these FBI interviews conclusive identifications had not yet been made of Layton and the others who had, in fact, died at Jonestown. Within this file of interviews Layton is variously described as one of the "insiders who might have knowledge of some contingency plans"; one of the "confidants and ranking members"; along with twenty-two others as "dangerous and on the personal staff of Peoples Temple"; and as "being knowledgeable of Peoples Temple operations." On a more sinister note Layton is described as "very dangerous"; a member of a group of eleven who "had a pact that if anyone left they would be hunted down and have their throat cut"; and that she had "planned the murders of the Peoples Temple defectors."[5]

All of these interviews must certainly be understood within the

4. Although the reports, which were obtained from the FBI through the Freedom of Information Act, are all anonymous, many of the interviewees provide details about the length of time they were involved in Peoples Temple and the circumstances under which they left the group.

5. All quotes are from FBI, Guyana Evidence Index, 89-4286.

context of the kinds of "atrocity" stories, reviewed previously, that defectors from religious groups often tell. Certainly a heightened level of fear and anxiety must have been at work for those who had been involved with people who had died so dramatically. Yet, even the interviewee who told of Layton being involved in the group that would hunt down and cut the throats of people, mentions four women —Carolyn Layton, Sandy Bradshaw, Linda Amos, and Karen Layton (Larry Layton's second wife)—as having "all available inside information to Jones's operation and were devout followers as well as his mistresses." One report, from a man who described himself as being very active in Peoples Temple, identified Carolyn Layton as among the "very strong supporters of Peoples Temple" and "very powerful in the organization," then adds that she could be the "next leader for the Peoples Temple." Even for those people for whom Peoples Temple represented danger there was an acknowledgment that it was possible for a woman in leadership to both have authority and be sexually involved with Jones simultaneously. The latter did not cancel out the former for people who had been members of Peoples Temple and had experienced the power practiced by Jones and these women.

"When I was in Peoples Temple I had more power that I'll ever again attain in my life." These are the words of Grace Stoen Jones some fourteen years after the tragedy at Jonestown that claimed the life of her son and many friends. (Ironically, Grace Stoen married a man whose last name is Jones, so that her name is now Grace Stoen Jones. To avoid confusion, however, I call her Grace Stoen, the name by which she was known during her years of involvement with the Temple.) Grace Stoen was a part of the cadre of young, dynamic white women who were active in the leadership of Peoples Temple during the expansion and optimism that marked the Redwood Valley and early San Francisco years. Although I am critical of women's status in the Temple being described primarily in terms of their relationships with husbands, lovers, or, particularly, Jim Jones, in the case of Grace Stoen it is an accurate statement (and not merely a reflection of an ideological schema) that her involvement in Peoples Temple was contingent upon her relationship with her husband, Timothy Oliver Stoen. Tim Stoen was already a practicing lawyer and had been attending Peoples Temple for more than one year when he began dating Grace Grech, who was twelve years his junior. Her involvement in the leadership of Peoples Temple had as much to do with her marriage to Tim Stoen as it had to do with any particular skills or talents she brought to the organization. Nonetheless, she quickly discovered that the administrative skills she had acquired as a secretary before joining the Temple were in high demand in the bureaucratically sophisticated world of Peoples Temple.

When I met Grace Stoen in 1992 at the fourteenth anniversary memorial service at Evergreen Cemetery in Oakland where more than two hundred of the unidentified and unclaimed members of the Jonestown dead are buried, I was impressed by her intense, rapid-fire articulation of her views on what had happened in Peoples Temple during her six years of active membership. During my interviews with her in the weeks that followed the service it was clear that she is a woman who wants her motives for having been involved in Peoples Temple to be understood (interviews with the author 3, 7 Dec. 1992). This desire is more clearly appreciated when one recalls that her son, John Victor Stoen, was at the center of the custody battle that heightened the paranoia of Jonestown and focused the efforts of the Concerned Relatives group. Her grief over the loss of this small boy still deeply moves and haunts her. The 1992 memorial service was the first of those annual services that Grace Stoen attended. Her son's body is buried at Evergreen Cemetery.

Although she lost her son and many friends at Jonestown and might, therefore, have been expected to speak with uniform negativity of her experience in Peoples Temple, she spoke of those six years of involvement with a kind of nostalgia. Despite Stoen's active involvement in Concerned Relatives and her role as occasional spokesperson for the anticult movement her straightforward narrative included both negative and, surprisingly, positive judgments on Peoples Temple activities and members. My overall impression was that Stoen wanted to give me all the information she had in the hope that I might sort it out and help her to make sense of the experience. When asked about the role of women in the Temple, she stated that women were given "all the respect, all the power" within the inner circle of leaders. There was a feeling of power and influence that the young women in leadership, including herself, had never experienced before. She spoke of how exhilarating it was to be actively involved in offering care and respect to black people, the elderly, and children; how important she felt in offering protection to people who were "in danger" in society. She talked about what an incredible educational experience it was to be involved in Peoples Temple during the Redwood Valley days. No sooner was a social problem identified than the Temple set about contributing its energy and resources toward solving it. She can remember thinking at the time, "No where else is this happening."

A special concern of the Temple that attracted Stoen was the plight of the elderly. Jim Jones often preached about how the elderly lacked the financial resources to care for themselves physically, but even more damaging to their self-esteem was how the American capitalist society that values money and youth strips individuals of their dignity as they grow older. Grace Stoen learned that she had a gift for empathizing with people, especially the elderly. She could see what a difference it made in the life of an elderly person to be respected and taken seriously. During her time in Peoples Temple she first worked in a convalescent hospital, later became engaged in the organizational administration of Peoples Temple in Redwood Valley, and later still worked in the counseling program of the Temple. Eventually, she became head counselor, a job she held from 1973 to 1976.

While Grace Stoen was speaking about the people of Peoples Temple, especially Jim Jones, her face was clouded with sadness as she looked down at her hands, rarely making eye contact. When she did so, her eyes were often brimming with tears. What a striking contrast in her self-presentation when, during the same interview, she began speaking about the actual work she did at the Redwood Valley office of the Temple. She became animated, and her voice took on a strength I had not heard before. Her enthusiasm for the work itself—what she was able to accomplish and the authority she exercised—was clear not just in what she said but in the way she said it. From 1974 to 1976 Stoen managed the office in Redwood Valley and was in charge of acquiring passports for all the members of the Peoples Temple who emigrated to Guyana. Having spent many hours at the California Historical Society, Peoples Temple Archives, looking through these passport applications, I have a sense of the magnitude of this job. Many of the people who moved to Jonestown were born in the southern United States near the turn of the twentieth century and had no record of their births. Some knew little more than the state they had been born in. Stoen had to acquire the documentation for each individual, if available, and to obtain legal waivers for documents, if not. Grace Stoen was in the office answering the phone and working on the passport project routinely from 8:00 in the morning until the early hours of the following morning. She also worked on the accounts payable for the publishing arm of the Temple and oversaw the maintenance of the fleet of buses that the church had acquired for its trips to

San Francisco and Los Angeles. The heart of the Temple before its move to San Francisco in 1975 was the office that Grace Stoen managed in Redwood Valley.

As the political and mission emphasis of the Temple shifted to the urban environment of San Francisco, Stoen's activities focused increasingly on counseling, rather than administration. When a person in the Temple had a problem of any kind—emotional, interpersonal, financial, drug-related, sexual, even spiritual—Stoen's job was to get the "complaint" in writing (or write it herself), then to pass these letters along to the staff of counselors who would work with the person or family, often on the same day. It was not rare for Stoen to be handling fifty such counseling needs at any given time. Often she would simply work with the person herself although her job as head counselor was to be a resource manager, not a counselor. Debbie Layton Blakey, who worked with Grace Stoen during this period, described Stoen as having the "personal qualities of generosity and compassion [that] made her very popular with the membership" (Rose 1979, 170).

Stoen spoke in great detail about how her position as head counselor affected her relationship with Jim Jones and with the larger Peoples Temple community. She understood that her "job" was to be a "buffer to keep people from Jim Jones." Because many of the people involved in the community had first been attracted to it because of the charismatic authority of Jones, when they had a problem they wanted him to address it personally. Stoen's admittedly difficult task was to keep people away from Jones while conveying to them that Jones in fact cared (and cared deeply) about them personally and would have been happy to have counseled them if that had been possible. At the same time she felt that she had to be careful not to "flaunt" the access that she had to Jones in front of the other members, especially the other women, in the leadership circle. Stoen spoke of her head counseling job as "the most power I will ever have in my life" because she could decide who saw Jim Jones and who did not, whose problems were a priority and whose were not. Certainly, Stoen was fulfilling a very important "gatekeeping" function for Jones, filtering and distilling importing information about the community for the leader's consumption and working as a "communications officer," transmitting information from the leader in an informal way back into the community. Both organizational functions were explored in the "sex and power" schema developed in chapter 3. She was intimate with Jones emotionally but whether the intimacy included sex only Grace Stoen knows. Perhaps the fact of sex is not as important in this analysis as is the *belief* that a sexual relationship was taking place. That belief would have initiated the "sex and power" organizational dynamic and put Stoen in a position to serve as gatekeeper and communications officer. Certainly, the members of Peoples Temple assumed sexual intimacy between Jones and Stoen, an assumption confirmed by Tim Stoen's affidavit about the paternity of John Victor. Shortly after the birth of John Victor Stoen, Timothy Oliver Stoen signed a statement, along with Marceline Jones, claiming that Jim Jones was the father of John Victor and that he had asked Jones to have a child with Grace Stoen so that his child would be fathered by "the most compassionate, honest, and courageous human being the world contains" (Reiterman 1982), 131).

One of the primary group building tools that Jim Jones used was inclusion-exclusion. Stoen was ambiguous about whether Jones manipulated people consciously with a desire to control their behavior for his own aggrandizement or if he simply had a gift for understanding what motivated people—especially women, Stoen pointed out—and was able to channel those motivations toward the ministries of Peoples Temple. (She made both arguments at various times in interviews with me.) Stoen described the inclusion-exclusion dynamic as "nobody wanted to be left out or left behind." According to Stoen, the women in leadership were particularly willing to sacrifice—sleep, money, or sex—to demonstrate their loyalty to Peoples Temple and the causes to which it was committed. The worst possible charge was to be accused of elitism in this self-consciously socialist group. She remembers Jones saying repeatedly in the Planning Commission and to chosen individuals that the "real religious work harder." Thus, in a manner not unlike the dynamic that Max Weber (1958) identified as being central to the motivation of seventeenth century Protestants in America, the people (particularly the women) within the leadership of Peoples Temple were at pains to prove they were the "real religious" and not merely going through the motions. Thus, loyalty to apostolic socialism, the blend of Christianity and Marxism upon which Peoples Temple theology was based (see chapter 1), became a kind of litmus test for how deeply and genuinely these women in leadership had forsaken their elitist upbringing, education, and social orientation.

The Planning Commission was the official leadership body of Peoples Temple. The "inner circle" or "leadership circle" referred to here was a more informal group of Peoples Temple leaders. All of them, including Carolyn Layton, were in the Planning Commission but held more authority with Jones and in the movement than membership in the Planning Commission conferred. Hall (1987) indicates that Jones was surrounded by three tiers of leaders: confidants, administrators, and the Planning Commission. All served the "client population," or the rank and file Peoples Temple members (see also Weightman 1983, chap. 3).

Because Peoples Temple was charismatically led, loyalty to the group's ideals became entwined with loyalty to Jim Jones himself. According to Stephan Jones, his father knew that he could manipulate the people around him precisely because of their commitment to the Peoples Temple ministry. Jones believed that the end justified the means, which meant that he was continually asking people in his movement to override the boundaries of what they felt was appropriate because it was "good for Peoples Temple." Even outrageous behavior on the part of Jones was interpreted as a lesson, and the people around him would ask "what is he [Jones] trying to show us?" (S. G. Jones interview, 7 Dec. 1992).

Stoen stated that women worked harder in Peoples Temple because they knew that dedication and commitment would be rewarded with influence and power. Although she called Peoples Temple a "racist organization," she nonetheless asserted that "any person could have power in Peoples Temple." Peoples Temple was a two-tiered organization: the majority of members were black and had only minimal formal education; those in leadership were almost exclusively white and well-educated.[6] It was almost impossible for black persons to make their way into positions of influence in the Temple, and in that sense Peoples Temple was both racist and institutionally inflexible. Yet if individuals got into the leadership circle (being young, white, educated, and female increased one's chances) only the limits of individual loyalty and commitment stood in the way of achieving authority in the organization. Thus, it was Grace Stoen's impression that "in society men were in power, but in Peoples Temple women were given the honor and power." Further, she pointed out that over the years of her involvement this power differential between men and women in-

6. In chapter 5 I address this split and suggest that Peoples Temple was actually three groups in one organization and that the tension these fissures produced contributed to the decision to commit suicide.

creased until by the time she left in July 1976 men were routinely "put down and cut down" in casual conversation and women were spoken of as "stronger both physically and emotionally, with longer lives to prove it."

Stoen pointed out that one thing Jones did especially well in his relationships with women in leadership was to make them feel "valued and beautiful." This approach was particularly effective with women who were intelligent and well educated, but who doubted themselves as sexually attractive women. Stoen named Carolyn Moore Layton as someone who fit this description. According to Stoen, Jones used sex to draw people in and make them feel special, which had the effect (although she was ambiguous about whether this was Jones's intention) of increasing their commitment to the movement and loyalty to him personally. She described Layton as someone for whom "power didn't mean much. Love was what motivated her" (G. S. Jones interview, 3 Dec. 1992).

Stephan Jones believes that his father knew full well that his having sex with the women in leadership had the effect of "hooking them in." He witnessed his father use this strategy with most of the women in leadership although with one notable exception. Jones refused to have a sexually intimate relationship with Sharon (Linda) Amos because her "unrequited desire" would fuel more loyalty than if he slept with her. Stephan Jones expressed admiration for the commitment of Carolyn Layton, Maria Katsaris, and Sharon Amos but pointed out that they became dangerous people when that "commitment was coupled with a high degree of self-deception." They did not believe that "they were enough in themselves," nor did they have enough "self-confidence and inner security" to recognize that Jones needed them as much as they needed Jones (S. G. Jones interview, 19 Dec. 1992).[7]

Chris Hatcher, chair of the Join Federal/State/Local Task Force on the Peoples Temple/Jonestown mass suicide/murder and clinical professor of psychology at the University of California, San Francisco, clarifies how complex the connections between love and power were for the women of Peoples Temple. In his work with survivors of Jonestown he found that both men and women in the leadership shared

7. Stephan Jones survived the suicides because he and some of the other young men from Jonestown were in Georgetown playing in a basketball tournament during Congressman Ryan's visit.

a "rush" as they successfully addressed seemingly intractable social problems, such as racism and poverty. This rush was not unlike the heart-expanding sensation one experiences when falling deeply and suddenly in love. Hatcher described this feeling as "enormously intox-icating," especially for women because "Jim Jones offered women more responsibility and power than they would have had in the outside world" (Hatcher interview, 1 Dec. 1992). Within Peoples Temple, the women in leadership had the authority to influence the social prob-lems about which they were most concerned.

Eileen MacDonald, a journalist who conducted a series of person-to-person interviews with women engaged as terrorists in revolution-ary struggles, confirmed the words of Grace Stoen and Hatcher about the energy and commitment that women bring to the causes they love. She observed that there was a large difference between what she had read about the participation of women in terrorist organizations and her experience of the role they played.

> I read that women usually only played support roles in such groups, probably as girlfriends to the men. However, it quickly became clear that while the men did a lot of talking and planning, it was the women who met up late at night to carry out the actions. They seemed to have more energy and commitment than the men, and were prepared to risk more. (MacDonald 1991, 1)

Indeed, the title of the book from which the passage above is quoted, *Shoot the Women First*, comes from the advice given to new recruits in antiterrorist forces.

Once inside the group, MacDonald discovered that "not only were women members in the majority, they were also, in effect, its leaders." She began to wonder why there was so little recognition outside anti-terrorism circles of the leadership positions that women held in these groups. She concluded "if the male members of a movement commit-ted to violence are seen as mad, bad and evil, how much more the females? In taking up arms they commit a double atrocity: using vio-lence, and in the process destroying our safe, traditional view of women" (MacDonald 1991, 4).

This latter "atrocity" is by far the worst, for it creates a feeling of ambivalence in nonrevolutionary society. On the one hand, society hates these women for destroying its hopes that women will redeem the world through their role as "protectors and givers of life," while, on the other hand, it is attracted to a woman who scorns all the norms of society and risks her life in a seemingly hopeless cause because she believes so passionately in its justness. As MacDonald points out, "Such figures appeal to the rebel in all of us—just because they are dangerous, have stepped out of bounds" (MacDonald 1991, 8). It is their danger, both as potential role models for young women and as destroyers of an illusion about the essential moral superiority of women, which has caused their role in these organizations—and, I argue, in Peoples Temple as well—to be filtered out of the narratives about these groups.

MacDonald observed that women in these revolutionary groups had this increased level of commitment and potential for violence because they were forced to be "doubly tough" due to the gender stereotyped assumptions of men in their movement. The women had to be "constantly on their guard against any emotion that might be construed as "feminine weakness," and this might further explain why they are on occasion more ruthless. Newly acquired power and status, especially if vulnerable and on trial, is heady and exciting in itself, and may induce overreaction in a crisis" (MacDonald 1991, 237).

In addition, the women were in a position from which it was less likely, or even possible, for them to return to mainstream society and to resume "normal" lives. Losing the cause was not an option for them because they had committed the "double deviance" of being perceived both as "brutal animals" and "unnatural women" (MacDonald 1991, 238). A woman is more loyal to the cause to which she has committed and more extreme in demonstrating that loyalty because of the greater sacrifice she has made in joining the group combined with a need to prove she is not less willing to be violent or to suffer deprivation because she is female.

The loyalty which the women in leadership in Peoples Temple felt was made infinitely more complex, both emotionally and organizationally, by the fact that their commitment to the cause was directly associated with the person Jim Jones. The desire to change the world and the attraction for the individuals involved in that enterprise became entwined and confused within the leadership. To love God's justice here on earth was to love Jim Jones; to be loyal to socialist values was to be loyal to Jim Jones. Any betrayal of Jones thus became a betrayal of the community and all it stood for.[8] Stephan Jones de-

8. For the significance of this loyalty/betrayal dynamic see chapter 7.

scribed Carolyn Moore Layton, for example, as having two primary motivations that were inextricably connected, "She loved Jim Jones and she wanted to change the world" (S. G. Jones interview, 7 Dec., 1992). Layton herself, in a letter to her sister Rebecca, clarified these two motivations when she wrote about Jones, "He has given my life meaning and purpose and most importantly love" (Moore 1986, 69).

Hatcher points out that this love and loyalty for the movement and for individual(s) involved did not flow only from the women in leadership to Jim Jones but from Jones to the women as well. According to Hatcher, Jones knew how important the women were to Peoples Temple. In fact, it "could not have existed without the women" (Hatcher interview, 1 Dec. 1992). As a result, it is possible to speculate that not only were these women "falling in love" with the movement/Jones but also that Jones was "in love" with the movement/women. Especially this must have been the case with Carolyn Moore Layton, who was central to Peoples Temple and, later, to Jonestown's management.

Stephan Jones was aware that Carolyn Layton behaved as "a wife" to his father as early as 1969 when Stephan was only 10 years old. He grew up aware of Layton's central role in his father's life. She was Jim Jones's "favorite," and that position was never challenged, no matter how much philandering his father engaged in. Stephan Jones resented and disliked her because of how her presence in their lives hurt his mother. As the stress mounted at Jonestown, however, he grew to appreciate the amount of pressure she was under and how well she kept her fear and despair "under wraps." He also knew that she felt guilty about the affair but was utterly committed to her relationship with Jim Jones. Stephan recalled that Layton preferred to work "behind the scenes" and was generally "passive" in public meetings of the Temple. At the same time, he remembered her impatience that "all previous methods of achieving social justice, for example, passive resistance, had not worked." His father was a "charismatic and dynamic man" who "swept Carolyn Layton off her feet" (S. G. Jones interview, 7 Dec. 1992).

Within the field of new religious movements charismatic authority as a characteristic of the management style of these groups has gotten the lion's share of attention, in part because it is a visible difference between new religions and mainstream religious organizations that rely on bureaucratic authority. Max Weber has been particularly influential in identifying the sociological dynamics of charismatic authority. Three aspects of Weber's understanding of charisma are relevant to understanding the relationship between Jones and his inner circle. First, charisma only translates into power when it is recognized by others.

> Charisma is self-determined and sets its own limits. Its bearer seizes the task for which he is destined and demands that others obey and follow him by virtue of his mission. *If those to whom he feels sent do not recognize him, his claim collapses;* if they recognize it, he is their master as long as he "proves" himself. (Weber 1978, 1112–13, italics added)

Weber is suggesting a two-way flow of power between the charismatic leader and his followers. The leader is only able to influence the movement he has founded as long as the followers were willing to acknowledge the special status of the leader's authority. This authority is unique to the leader and is highly personal. "The bearer of charisma enjoys loyalty and authority by virtue of a mission believed to be embodied in him" (Weber 1978, 1117). Therefore, proximity to the charismatic leader becomes a highly coveted position within the group.

This desire to be close to the source of power is invested with a kind of urgency because of another characteristic: "charismatic authority is naturally unstable" (Weber 1978, 1114). There is constant pressure on the leader to confirm the follower's faith in him and to use his unique authority to provide well-being and safety for the community. Because it is always possible for the followers to withdraw their support, and the threat of this hangs over the leader's head like Damocles's sword, charismatic authority is always, from its genesis, in the process of routinizing. The charismatic leader himself may be of two minds about this drift toward bureaucratization. On the one hand, it takes the pressure off having to perform miracles and provide well-being for the community single-handedly. On the other hand, it means relinquishing status in the community.

Third, Weber indicates that it is the inner circle, or "disciples," of the charismatic leader and his followers who have the most to gain by "the routinization of charisma."

> Thus the pure type of charismatic rulership is in a very specific sense unstable, and all its modifications have basically one and the same

cause: The desire to transform charisma and charismatic blessing from a unique, transitory gift of grace of extraordinary times and persons into a permanent possession of everyday life. This is desired usually by the master, *always by his disciples*, and most of all by his charismatic subjects. (Weber 1978, 1121, italics added)

Weber does not precisely spell out why this routinization is desirable for the charismatic leader's followers, other than noting the desire to make charisma universally available. (As Weber points out, this is the beginning of the end for charismatic authority in any event.) There is a kind of intrinsic unfairness to charismatic authority: the leader cannot always ensure the instant delivery of what is needed by the group, a fact that his most intimate followers must attempt to interpret to the rank and file. One way to avoid this uncomfortable position is to make the "delivery" of what is needed by the rank and file members more predictable and universal. Certainly, this was the case with Jim Jones's waning ability to provide "divine healings" for his followers. At first, in the early California years, he was aided in these healings by loyal followers who helped fabricate the healings (Weightman 1983, 130–32). The justification for this deception was that a faked healing might inspire a real one and that once people became members of Peoples Temple they would realize that socialism was the priority, not healings. Basically, it was a transfer of power from Jones himself to his inner circle, who were providing these "healings," such as they were, and knew that Jones had not performed them himself. Later, there was a shift away from Jones and his healings to the scientific medical care that Peoples Temple nurses and doctor could provide, predictably and universally, without depending at all on Jones.

Jones's management style flowed from and supported his "charisma" and the love/power dynamic that existed between himself and his most intimate female followers. According to Hatcher, Peoples Temple was a "task-oriented" rather than a "role-oriented" organization. This orientation contributed to the degree of flexibility that Jones and his top staff exercised within the organization (Hatcher interview, 1 Dec. 1992). This is how, for example, Grace Stoen could move from administration to counseling in the space of one day. Because one's authority and responsibilities could be changed in an instant, without any reasons being offered, a kind of anxiety and instability was associated with being in leadership. One way of ensuring (as much as was possible) that one would continue to be assigned important tasks was to reaffirm one's loyalty by dedicating more time and financial resources to the movement. Another way to solidify one's authority was to have sex with Jim Jones. The incentive for having authority within Peoples Temple was the rush intrinsic in completing tasks successfully, especially tasks that met the needs of people, such as the elderly and poor and urban blacks who were the central focus of the Peoples Temple ministry. These people had become accustomed to being neglected and mistreated and their gratitude for the attention and help they received from Peoples Temple was often overwhelming to those who provided it, according to both Grace Stoen and Stephan Jones.

Task-oriented organizations provide an emotional high for those involved in a way that role-oriented organizations never can. The duties of a more bureaucratically organized group with job descriptions and role expectations are more uniformly spread out and more predictable; therefore, the institutional rewards are less frequent and more mundane. By contrast, being in leadership in Peoples Temple was a bit like gambling. Much was at stake, and the winnings, when they came, were large. Hatcher pointed out that Jones had consistently, from Indiana up to the final days of Jonestown, "flown by the seat of his pants" as leader of Peoples Temple. He became accustomed to voicing ideas, many of them not well thought out, then having the women in leadership figure out a way for them to be done. This encouraged creativity on the part of those in the inner circle and caused Jones to depend utterly on the women in leadership for getting anything done (Hatcher interview, 1 Dec. 1992). Is it possible, then, to argue that Jones was as much in thrall to the women in leadership as they were to him?

There was a time in 1977 when, according to David Chidester, Jim Jones decided that the Jonestown community should abstain from sex. Chidester, without documenting any evidence, suggests that this period lasted for three to four months. He quotes Jones as saying, "What we ought to be at this revolutionary stage is no sex, including the leader" (Chidester 1988b, 102). This is a tantalizing scenario, given what I have suggested. Perhaps Jones was feeling vulnerable about the kind of power that the women he was having sex with were holding in the community, so decided to place a moratorium on sexual relations.

Over the years Jones had developed a philosophy about sexuality for the Peoples Temple community. He suggested that there were three reasons to have sex: to prevent treason, to facilitate growth, and to experience pleasure. Chidester comments,

> His self-proclaimed sexual prowess had been responsible, he occasionally pointed out, for solidifying the loyalties of many of the members of the inner leadership circle of the Peoples Temple. And when some of those trusted associates betrayed him by defecting from the Temple, Jones tended to explain their treason as a result of his refusal to have sex with them. (Chidester 1988b, 103)

What Chidester and the people I interviewed suggest is a situation in Peoples Temple that was just the opposite from the all too frequently used "sex in cults" schema. Rather than love/sex erasing the power of the women involved, the presence of these, in fact (within the context of the group), enhanced both their power and that of Jim Jones. The ideological assumptions that undergird the "sex in cults" view of Jonestown are that the women in the leadership of Peoples Temple were first and foremost sexual beings and their institutional authority was not centrally relevant to the success (or, later, the failure) of the movement and that Jones's power was not at all dependent upon his sexual involvement with the women in leadership, which was merely an expression of his "natural" male desires or the intrinsic depravity of charismatic leadership. I suggest that sexuality and love in the Peoples Temple were expressions of loyalty and commitment between the women in leadership and Jones, who represented Peoples Temple and the hope for a just world, *and* were the foundation for Jones's authority in the movement through the power these women exercised as conduits, information officers, and managers of the various tasks in which Peoples Temple was engaged.

5

Three Groups in One

Since Ernst Troeltsch's groundbreaking work (1931) on the relationship between church and society in which he defined *church* and *sect* as two different kinds of religious bodies that have a number of theological and demographic traits, sociologists of religion have felt obliged to define their use of these terms before applying them to specific religious groups. Some have defined them on the basis of theological views or the dynamics of the group's sociohistorical origins, others on the basis of demographics, yet others by the classic Troeltschian typology.[1] To add to the confusion around these categories, which have even less uniformity of application than of definition, a "new" kind of religious group appeared on the American social landscape in the 1960s, which has been variously described as "new religious movements," "innovative religions," "marginal religions," or more commonly, "cults." The difficulty with using this latter term is that it has been used pejoratively by the anticult movement and sensationally by the media so that it is no longer clear that it can be used as a neutral descriptive term in social scientific inquiry. For this reason I use *new religious movement* to refer to this latter category.

One of the weaknesses of the analyses of the Jonestown suicides to date has been the tendency to explore only Jim Jones's motive, then treat the group as a uniform mass as in "mass suicide." By looking at the three groups that existed side by side within Peoples Temple and exploring the motives for each one gains an insight into the complex

1. Thomas O'Dea 1966 is the most thorough exploration of the Troeltschian model.

nature of the decision to commit suicide on 18 November 1978.[2] I argue that a membership shift occurred when Peoples Temple relocated to California, which caused Peoples Temple to become first two, then later three, groups within a single movement. The Indiana Peoples Temple was essentially a sect, which was joined by new religious movement members in California, which then recruited black church members as it focused its ministry on the residents of urban California. Each group had its own organizational role in Peoples Temple—with the California new religious movement members holding the most institutional power—and its own understanding of the purpose and meaning of Jonestown.

Stark and Bainbridge (1985, chap. 2) stress the issue of the sociohistorical origins of a religious group when distinguishing among churches, sects, and cults. To Stark and Bainbridge a sect is a religious organization that has broken away from another religious group over issues of belief or leadership, whereas a cult is a group that arises out of the general social environment because of a religious or spiritual innovation that is attractive to a number of people. In addition they stress the importance of the relationship between the religious movement being studied (whether church, sect, or cult) and the surrounding sociocultural environment. Their theory, building on that of Benton Johnson (1963), is that a church is in relatively low tension with its host society, whereas both sects and cults are in high tension. The difference between sects and cults is based on the origination factor: sects split off of already existing groups, whereas cults are born of an innovaton in belief or practice or both that captures the imagination of some people.

The Indiana Sect

The Indiana-based Peoples Temple Full Gospel Church was a sect both in terms of its origins and its own self-concept. Jim Jones was not claiming to have created something new with Peoples Temple. Rather,

---

2. By examining the specific historical and sociological details of Jonestown it is more difficult to apply the "lesson of Jonestown," which generally boils down to "all cults are bad," to the great variety of new religions. One of my intentions in this discourse is to make it more difficult for those who want to destroy new religions on ideological or theological grounds to do so by recourse to the "this group is a Jonestown waiting to happen" argument.

he was calling his followers back to the "authentic" Christianity reflected in the ministry of Jesus Christ to the outcasts of society. As Stark and Bainbridge point out, "Sects claim to be the authentic, purged, refurbished version of the faith from which they split" (1979, 125). After several years of attempting to integrate racially the Methodist Church in Indianapolis as a student pastor, Jim Jones gave up on mainstream institutional Protestantism and decided to initiate a church that was "truer" to the Gospel message of love and inclusiveness. In 1954 Jones rented a building in a racially mixed area of Indianapolis, which he named Community Unity. The success of that ministry, which focused on Pentecostal-style healing services, free meals for the poor and homeless, and nursing home facilities for the elderly, was followed by a move to a bigger church in another racially mixed inner-city neighborhood where Wings of Deliverance metamorphosed into Peoples Temple. By 1960 twenty-eight hundred meals per month were being served by Peoples Temple under the direction of Reverend Archie Ijames, the first black man to be in leadership in the sect (Reiterman 1982, 55).[3] In Indiana, Jones initiated a leadership structure that involved a team of ministers, including Russell Winberg and Jack Beam from the Laurel Street Tabernacle and Archie Ijames.

"Divine" healings, clairvoyance, and other demonstrations of special spiritual gifts were Jim Jones's drawing card during the late 1950s in Indiana. He attracted several families from the Laurel Street Tabernacle—the Cordell family was among these early Pentecostal recruits—and nearly twenty people from a spiritualist state convention at which he demonstrated his psychic gifts (Reiterman 1982, 50). Edith Parks began attending Peoples Temple because of her positive impression of Jones from that convention, and she eventually brought into the Temple her son, daughter-in-law, and grandchildren. The Cordells and Parks relocated with Peoples Temple twice, once to California and then to Guyana. The Parks family were important core members of the Indiana sect with skills and dedication to offer the growing religious movement. Dale Parks, one of Edith's grandchildren, was an inhalation therapist whose medical training was especially important for the health care of the large population of elderly who moved with Peoples Temple to Jonestown. Tim Reiterman notes that it was

3. According to CHS, BB-18-z-78, the restaurant on N. Delaware Street in Indianapolis first opened its doors on 24 February 1960 and fed eighteen people; the second day it fed one hundred until it leveled off at twenty-eight hundred per month.

Marceline Jones who convinced Dale Parks to relocate to Guyana: "Dale had become disenchanted with Jones in California; however, Marceline Jones pleaded with him to give Jonestown a chance" (393).

Marceline Jones was an important leader within the Indiana sect and one of the reasons for its success. The nursing homes that Peoples Temple established were a particular interest of Marceline Jones, who was trained as a nurse and had a fondness for working with older people. Reiterman writes of her commitment to this ministry during the Indiana years. "When [the Joneses] found one of the Temple members unhappy and covered with bedsores in a nursing home, they brought the woman to their large white duplex. . . . Marceline converted her own house into a nursing home, with help from Jim, and, while working an outside nursing job, brought the home up to state standards" (Reiterman 1982, 56). The two nursing homes that Marceline Jones ran in Indianapolis were known for their high standards of care. The ratio of aides to residents was high, and there was a commitment to no differentiation between the paying and nonpaying patients.[4]

Marceline Jones's importance as a Christian role model extended beyond her nursing care for the elderly to the matriarch of a "rainbow family." The Joneses referred to themselves in this way as they self-consciously attempted to model a racially integrated society within their own family (Hall 1987, 47–48). Starting in the late 1950s, she and Jim adopted two orphans from Korea, she gave birth to their only natural son, Stephan Gandhi Jones, and they adopted a black child, whom they named after his adoptive father. They were the first white couple in Indianapolis to adopt a black child (47–48). The Indiana sect that the Joneses founded was very much a family affair. When Wings of Deliverance was incorporated in April 1955, Jim, Marceline, and Jim's mother, Lynetta Jones, were the trustees (43). Marceline Jones was as committed to its social justice ministry as was Jim. When Jones began preaching about feeding the hungry and taking care of the sick, the numbers in attendance at services began to fall off. But Marceline Jones was undaunted: "People that did stay were people that wanted to go on to perfection. . . . And so where numbers were sacrificed, quality was gained" (45).

Jones encouraged members of Peoples Temple to refer to himself as "father" and to Marceline as "Mother Jones." This reflected, in

4. CHS, BB-18-z-114.

part, the influence that Father Divine's Philadelphia-based interracial religious movement had on Jones. The Joneses had visited Father and Mother Divine in the 1950s and had been impressed with their social justice ministry and the organization of the movement. As C. Eric Lincoln has pointed out, referring to Marceline as "Mother" reflected the importance of her role in Peoples Temple: "Like Father Divine, Jones urged his parishioners in Indianapolis to call him 'Father' or 'Dad.' . . . In the black religious tradition counterpart terminology may also be applied to the wife of the leader—especially if he himself is highly venerated and if she is considered properly complementary" (Lincoln and Mamiya 1980, 17).

The California New Religious Movement

Marceline Jones's influence and authority began to diminish once the sect moved to California and began to attract new religious movement members. By virtue of its migration from America's Midwest to California, Peoples Temple metamorphosed from a sect into a cult in Stark and Bainbridge's schema. In California its blend of Pentecostal revivalism, divine healings, charismatic leadership, and an interracial social gospel ministry indeed represented something "new vis-à-vis the other religious bodies of the society in question," which was experienced by the new converts as something "different, new, more advanced" (Stark and Bainbridge 1979, 125). The individuals who joined Peoples Temple during the late 1960s and early 1970s saw Jim Jones—not Jim and Marceline Jones—as the leader of the religious movement they were joining. Particularly after Carolyn Layton became the visible partner of Jim Jones from 1969 onward, the authority of Marceline Jones began to fade.

Grace Stoen indicated that Marceline Jones spent most of her time with the "peripheral" members of the Temple. These so-called peripheral members were primarily the Indiana sect members and many of the urban black church members who joined in the mid-1970s and grew to respect and love her as the gentle "mother" of their church. Within the leadership, comprising almost exclusively educated, white women from the new religious movement group, she was often "put down" in her absence, according to Stoen. Further, Marceline Jones was aware of her marginal status within the inner circle and avoided meetings of the leadership unless her presence was absolutely necessary. Marceline was a "nonentity" in Stoen's words (G. S. Jones interview, 3 Dec. 1992).

Kenneth Wooden's book on Jonestown (1981) is an exemplar of anticult movement ideology. One sign of its dependence on ideology over data is that it has no notes. No references are needed because the reader will provide the "ideological connectives" as proof to support Wooden's argument. He portrays Jim Jones as a sex maniac who uses both women and men to gratify his own lust for power and sex. It includes a detailed explication of how brainwashing was practiced in Peoples Temple. His primary source of information are the atrocity stories of Peoples Temple apostate Jeannie Mills who, along with her husband, founded the Human Freedom Center, an anticult deprogramming center. Because Wooden has sympathy for Marceline Jones, he quotes from Mills a speech of Marceline's that gives some insight into the shift in influence that she had experienced once the inner circle began forming around her husband.

> It's true that I have had to share my husband in the past, for the Cause. It was always painful for me because I love him very much, and just like everyone else, it's painful for me to see the person I love with someone else. Several years ago, Jim asked me for a divorce because I just couldn't make the adjustment to being married to a man who was also married to a Cause. At that time I had to do some serious introspection and decide on my priorities. I knew I didn't want to lose Jim, so I agreed that I would share him with people who needed to relate to the Cause on a more personal level. This has been a very difficult thing for me to live with, and it's caused me a lot of heartache. However, tonight, as I heard him pour out his heart to you, explaining the suffering he goes through when he has to use his body to serve the Cause, I realized that I have been very selfish. I want to make a public statement tonight that I am willing to share my husband for the Cause, and that I won't resent it any longer. (Wooden 1981, 43–44).

Carolyn Layton and Jim Jones began their affair in early 1969. The numbers of people involved in the Peoples Temple ministry rose markedly in the early 1970s, and the sense of the importance and scale of the ministry that Marceline and Jim Jones had created in Indiana some twenty years earlier grew with it. One could easily read the above, substituting *Carolyn* for *cause* in most instances. It suggests that not only did "Jim equal Peoples Temple" for many of the women in leadership but for Jim (and Marceline) *Carolyn* may have represented the *Cause!* Thus, "I just couldn't make the adjustment to being married to a man who was also married to a Cause/Carolyn" and "I want to make a public statement tonight that I am willing to share my husband for the Cause/with Carolyn, and that I won't resent it any longer." This last statement was a public armistice between Marceline Jones and Carolyn Layton. Stephan Jones indicated that there was a great deal of "resentment and dislike" of Layton among those people who respected and loved his mother because Layton often "behaved as a wife" to Jim Jones (S. G. Jones interview, 7 Dec. 1992). By calling a truce Marceline Jones cleared the way for Layton to practice more public authority in the Temple, gave the Indiana members permission to be loyal to what Peoples Temple had become, and took the moral and sacrificial high ground. It was Marceline Jones who demonstrated in her speech that night that loyalty to the Peoples Temple *cause* could cost a person her marriage, her pride, her rightful place in her own religious movement, and foreshadowed still greater sacrifices to come.

The inner circle only became an entity after both the numbers and the complexity of the ministries increased with the move to California. In 1966, the year after the move from Indiana, Peoples Temple had only 86 adult members. By 1968 the numbers had increased only to 136 although significantly this increase represented the addition of the young intellectual elite such as Timothy Oliver Stoen and Carolyn Moore Layton (Hall 1987, 65). As Hall points out, this was a significant turning point for the one-time Indiana sect: "The influx of a core of White, middle-class California college graduates and professionals like Stoen, social worker Linda Amos, the Mertles, and high school teacher Carolyn Moore Layton attracted others from relatively affluent sectors of society" (67).

The most important effect of the addition of the new religious movement members was that their organizational and bureaucratic talent catapulted the Peoples Temple ministry onto a totally different scale of operation. By the time the movement relocated to Guyana in 1977 Peoples Temple was able to boast an active membership of three thousand (Hall 1987, 69). The inner circle developed as a result of the need to coordinate the ministry activities of the Temple and also to protect and control that most precious of limited resources within Peoples Temple—Jim Jones.

As Weightman notes, beginning at this time, "such limited power and confidence as he chose to share was invested in a largely unofficial elite consisting primarily of women" (Weightman 1983, 135). Perhaps it was easier for Jones to focus his attention on the new religious movement members rather than on the Indiana sect members in part because their loyalty to him was not shared with Marceline. For the Indiana sect there was a loyalty to both Jim and Marceline Jones and to what their family represented. They had watched the rainbow family come into being and had been part of building the social justice and humanitarian care ministry from the ground up. To the new religious movement members the ministry of Peoples Temple and the leadership of Jim Jones was already in place—albeit on a small scale—which led to a tendency to "deify" Jones for what he articulated and symbolized.

The Urban Black Church

Most of the three thousand and the majority of those who moved with Peoples Temple to Jonestown, Guyana, were yet a third type of Peoples Temple member. They were primarily black and lived in urban California, particularly San Francisco and Los Angeles. The attraction of Peoples Temple for these former and current church members was the ability to bridge the gap between the other-worldly preaching of many black spiritualist church traditions and the concrete political activism of the black power political movements. These were people whose faith in the healing power of God and the church had been shaken, but not destroyed, by the deaths of Martin Luther King and Malcolm X and the relentless pressures of urban life. For these members the healing the Temple could provide was an important attraction. But, as Weightman has rightly indicated, this was not a recapitulation of the divine healings of Jones's Indiana days, rather the healings were more general than those had been. "There were other, additional kinds of appeal, but all of them cluster around the concept of healing—the healing of individual personal ills, whether they be physical, spiritual, or emotional; the healing of small groups, most importantly, families; and the healing of society through eradication of racial injustice and economic inequality" (Weightman 1983, 76).

One of the theoretical assumptions within the field of new religious movements that has negatively impacted the understanding of Peoples Temple has been the reliance on deprivation theory and social psychological interpretations of why people joined the movement. Deprivation theory has tended to focus on the socioeconomic needs of the urban blacks who joined Peoples Temple, whereas the social psychological schema has focused on the unmet emotional needs of the white elite from Indiana and California. In terms of the social psychological schema even the more educationally elite members were assumed to have some kind of problem that drove them to affiliate with a movement like Peoples Temple.

> According to the typical social psychological approach, the most likely recruits to cult organizations are persons who are relatively isolated, lacking in meaning and purpose, lower in social status, deprived, alienated, seeking simplistic solutions, and (as a result) susceptible to psychological manipulation. Such persons are assumed to be attracted to cults or sects because these groups promise purpose, security, love and social acceptance, status and satisfying roles, and communal solidarity. (Johnson 1979, 15)

The underlying assumption of either analysis is that nobody "normal," either economically comfortable or psychologically well-adjusted, would ever choose to become a member of a new religious movement. Even Steve Rose, a relatively sophisticated interpreter of Jonestown, refers to the majority of Peoples Temple members as "America's dispossessed underclass" (Rose 1979, 44) and "the largely helpless contingent of elderly blacks" (45), thus affirming their deprived status.

Weightman struggles against the deprivation theory schema by using exchange theorists James Downton and Rosabeth Moss Kanter to suggest that the urban black members of Peoples Temple did not have to be maladjusted to commit their lives to Peoples Temple nor to move to Jonestown, Guyana. Rather, their decision was the result of weighing the potential rewards and penalties of each action, which committed them more deeply to the group (Weightman 1983, chap. 2). Her more sophisticated application of deprivation theory suggests that there were fewer "penalties" in family and community disapproval for the socioeconomically disadvantaged who were attracted to Peoples Temple during its urban California membership drive and, potentially, much greater rewards in security and community. There was nothing "crazy" about those choices. On the contrary, given the social and economic conditions in which many urban blacks found themselves in San Francisco and Los Angeles during the 1970s, joining the Peoples Temple was a decidedly sane and rational decision.

Black scholars and pastors have tried to make sense of the attraction of Peoples Temple to Black Church members. C. Eric Lincoln and Lawrence Mamiya (1980) argue that Jones was able to see the unmet needs in the lives of urban blacks and offered an attractive religious alternative for those "individuals whose despair of relief has become increasingly pronounced and whose search for deliverance has turned from "rational" or conventional resources (which have been unavailing) to the challenge of possibilities which lie outside the normal pattern of social or ideological experience" (15).

They conclude that "it can be said of the Blacks who followed Jones . . . their common conviction is that they have finally found a way where there was no way" (Lincoln and Mamiya 1980, 16). This choice by individual Black Church members to become a follower of Jones actually led to a complete loss of self, according to Lincoln and Mamiya, as "the old unappreciated self is abandoned and the image of the believer is merged into the image of the cult" (16). The Black Church was severely shaken by the events at Jonestown. In the wake of the tragedy the question was posed: "Why, in this era of black consciousness and black liberation (in which the Black Church figures so prominently), so many black people did in fact give their allegiance, their money, and finally their lives to Jim Jones, a white, self-proclaimed apostle to America's disinherited" (8–9).

Lincoln and Mamiya find no satisfactory answer to this question but note that it is an area of inquiry that should interest and concern the Black Church.

Archie Smith, Jr., devoted the final chapter of his book on ethics and therapy from a Black Church perspective (1982) to a consideration of the "implications for the Black Church" of Peoples Temple and Jonestown. He points out that "a cross section of the black community was present at Jonestown—although the majority were from low-income neighborhoods, and many were welfare dependents" (A. Smith 1982, 196). He notes that some of the members of Peoples Temple were also members in good standing of their local Black Churches. Membership in Peoples Temple was not, according to Smith, necessarily a critique of the Black Church. He quotes one woman who was a member of both as saying that she joined Peoples Temple because "they did things together, ate and took trips together" (196). Like Lincoln, he sees the motivation for membership as having been a desire to escape "a general sense of despair that affects many in our society," specifically "loneliness, depression, exploitation, racism, alienation, sexism" (197). He commends the members of Peoples

Temple for not seeking refuge "in a privatized faith, but in a renewed and transformed social order" (179).

In the end Smith concludes that Jonestown was a "product of a culture which tends to repress and trivialize the essentially religious impulse" (A. Smith 1982, 207). Secularization is particularly problematic for black people because the connection between culture and religion has deep historic roots in the African experience. The community that Peoples Temple provided mirrored this connection and was, therefore, attractive to urban blacks for whom the three "key institutions" of black American survival—family, church, and religion —had ceased to provide a cohesive social environment (214).

> Black people's involvement in the Peoples' Temple Movement can be seen as an attempt to make black religion relevant to their social, political, and economic condition. By breaking with the insularity and seemingly irrelevant style of some recent black church worship, many thought they had found in the Peoples' Temple a form of church involvement that spoke more directly to the issues of spiritual uplift, justice, social empowerment, and change. (216).

Smith warns that there will be a temptation on the part of Black Church leaders to denounce Jones as a madman and his followers as victims without looking carefully at the implicit critique a predominantly black religious movement with an almost exclusively white leadership offers black mainstream religious organizations. Sadly, it seems that Smith was prophetic in predicting this response. At the fourteenth anniversary memorial service held at Evergreen Cemetery in Oakland, where the majority of the unclaimed Jonestown dead are buried, Evangelist Jynona Norwood described the two kinds of people who were attracted to Peoples Temple as "foolish or victims of circumstance."[5]

Unlike most scholars who have written about Peoples Temple, Archie Smith has focused on the demographic particularities of the people who were members. He includes at the end of his discussion two diagrams that detail the membership by gender, race, and age (A. Smith 1982, 229–31). He uses these demographics to make more

---

5. Jynona Norwood made these comments during the fourteenth anniversary memorial service, 18 November 1992, Evergreen Cemetery, Oakland, in which she demonized Jim Jones and portrayed the urban blacks within the Peoples Temple movement as victims of a madman.

explicit the point made by nearly every scholar who has studied Jones-town, namely, that Peoples Temple claimed to be reversing the racist social order but, in fact, perpetuated it within its own organization. The detail that he adds to this portrait, a portrait normally devoid of gender analysis, is that the 70 percent black membership was mostly women, many of whom were elderly (197).

One of the reasons why the membership numbers grew so rapidly during the mid-1970s was that Peoples Temple recruited entire family units and encouraged individual members to bring their families into the group (Weightman 1983, 86). Fifty women who were raising either one or two children without the support of a man were resident at Jonestown as were eighteen women with three or more children (see app. A, table 3). A great number of single individuals were there as well, but not the young, disaffected white people who are normally portrayed by the anticult movement as being attracted to new religions. Half of the three hundred single individuals at Jonestown were over the age of fifty, and nearly all of them were women (see app. A, table 4). The charge that new religious movements break up families has long been a foundational accusation of the anticult movement.[6]

Although Peoples Temple as a whole was more radical and, there-fore, in higher tension with the surrounding culture than was a typical church, the Temple, nonetheless, behaved like a traditional main-stream religious organization in its recruitment stategies. Its most ef-fective avenue for gaining new members was through the affective bonds of family and friends. This was true in its sect, new religious movement, and church phases. Individuals would be attracted to the Pentecostal-style healing services (this was especially the case in Indi-ana during the 1950s and 1960s), or interracial congregation and social activism (California during the late 1960s and early 1970s), or social services and supportive community (urban California during the mid-1970s). Individuals would then invite family members and close friends to participate in this wonderful church they had found. Even the most negative accounts of Peoples Temple generally start with an account of the excitement at having discovered such a lively, com-

6. This charge is probably used because much of the anticult movement's ideol-ogy and theory grew out of the battle that began in the 1970s between parents and their young adult children who had joined Unification Church, a new religious movement that included embracing Sun Myung Moon and his wife as "new parents" as a central part of its theology and social organization.

mitted, and caring congregation (Feinsod 1981, 89; Mills 1979, 117, 128–29).

The ministry in which the Peoples Temple new religious move-ment members were the most skilled was navigating the social welfare system in which many of its urban members found themselves entan-gled. This was especially appealing to those elderly members and single women with children who were dependent upon the government for financial assistance, housing, and health care. There are hundreds of files in the Peoples Temple Archives about social welfare or legal issues that Peoples Temple "counselors" helped members to negotiate. The goal of the mostly white and educated counselors was to protect their members from the dehumanization that poor, elderly, and black people often experience when dealing with government agencies. One of the shifts in ministry that occurred when Peoples Temple relocated to Jonestown was that instead of advocating on behalf of people against an existing bureaucratic system, the leadership found itself in a posi-tion of designing and administrating a bureaucratic system of their own, thus fulfilling Weber's prediction about the "routinization of charisma."

Throughout the history of Peoples Temple, no one was ever turned away no matter how great their problems. As a result, those in leader-ship were often overwhelmed with the economic, health, and emo-tional needs of members. Peoples Temple was proud of the number of criminals and drug addicts who were reformed through membership. Because Peoples Temple was committed religiously and politically to caring for anyone who came to them, there was an increased need to "control" those who did stay. In Jonestown this led to draconian measures. It also meant that the formula had been set that eventually led to attempting to meet unlimited needs with limited resources. This dilemma would be crucial in setting the stage for the psychic and social stress that led to the decision to commit suicide.

6

From Jones the Person
to Jonestown the Community

eoples Temple went through a period of rapid social change after
relocating to Jonestown, Guyana. Most interpreters of Peoples
Temple have commented on how the isolation of Jonestown promoted
dependence on Jim Jones and heightened the already well-developed
"insider-outsider" ideology of the organization. The shift that took
place, however, was actually more dramatic and quite different from
what this analysis suggests. I argue that the social change that occurred
within Peoples Temple because of the move to Jonestown actually
constituted a move *away* from Jim Jones's control rather than toward
greater dependence on him. Jones's power unraveled within his own
movement and authority shifted—perhaps including the authority to
carry out the suicides—from a combination of Jones and his leadership
circle to the leadership circle alone, specifically the women. The shift
was away from an emphasis on Jones to an emphasis on the Peoples
Temple community as a whole. It also solidified a transition in authority from the sect leaders to the new religious movement leaders that
had already substantively taken place during the outreach to urban
black church members in the early 1970s.

Jones's Shifting Authority

Jonathan Z. Smith has named the change that took place in the
move from California to Guyana as a shift from "subversive space" to
"utopian space" (J. Z. Smith 1982, chap. 7). Peoples Temple in California had provided for its members, especially its black church members, what the "establishment space" would not or could not. While

openly participating in political and religious activism, Peoples Temple was also, less visibly, organizing its own oppositional social system. "Internally, it was a counterpolis. It had its own modes of leadership, its own criteria for citizenship, its own mores and laws, its own system of discipline and punishment" (115).

There were aspects of this oppositional social system that the mainstream public was bound to object to once they learned of them, including disciplinary boxing matches, "catharsis" meetings, and faked healings and discernments. Jones himself admitted that deception was involved in some of the healings he performed. "People pass growths and then by sleight of hand I started doing it—and that would trigger others to get healed. It was kind of a catalyst process, to build faith" (Hall 1987, 20). In July 1977 *New West Magazine* (Kilduff and Tracy, 1977) published an article "Inside Peoples Temple" based upon the testimony of ten apostates which alleged that numerous abuses of power were taking place within Jones's organization. Most of the accusations centered on Jim Jones specifically and were interpreted by some as politically motivated because Jones up to that point had been a well-respected and powerful participant in the liberal San Francisco political establishment. Especially damaging were reports of abusive disciplinary proceedings during which a person who had violated a Peoples Temple policy was made to box with a stronger loyalist (Reiterman 1982, 259–60). There were also allegations of psychological abuse involving all night catharsis sessions during which members would "confess" to desires and behaviors ranging from homosexuality and child abuse to longing for more material things than were allowed under apostolic socialism (Hall 1987, 120–21). For Smith, Jones's move to Guyana was an exodus from the subversive space to the utopian precipitated by a recognition by the mainstream power structures that Peoples Temple was challenging race, class, age, and gender distinctions (J. Z. Smith 1982, 111).[1] Once the Peoples Temple subversion was widely known, it was bound to attract criticism that would make it difficult to continue to function in its dual role as both in and against mainstream society. The move to Jonestown was at least in part motivated by a desire to escape the close observation that the oppositional social system of People's Temple was beginning to attract.

1. Although more sensitive to the "ordinary humanness of the participants in Jonestown's White Night," Smith is still mostly concerned about Jim Jones in his analysis.

Doyle Paul Johnson, in a sociological analysis of the move to Jonestown, has suggested that charismatic leaders have historically chosen to relocate to isolated environments to consolidate their control over the group and to "avoid the contaminating and compromising influence of the wider society" (Johnson 1979, 318). Although it provides the desired social isolation, an unanticipated result of the move is that it actually weakens the leader's position in the group. In response to the demands of an environment in which shelter, food, and the other necessities of life must be provided by the group members the leader spends much of his time organizing mundane activities (321). His charismatic authority and ability to inspire the group members spiritually and emotionally weakens just when the members need motivation for the hard work required to keep the community going. Even if the leader successfully delegates the organizational duties of the religious movement, "some members' loyalty could be divided, and the original leader would no longer hold absolute sway over the group" (317).

Charismatic leadership is more important when a group is growing than when it is consolidating its life as a community. Therefore, Jones's leadership was more central in California than in Jonestown. Jones's importance as a leader was decreasing just when his capabilities as a community administrator were being put to the test. It was simply not possible for Jones to make all the decisions at Jonestown because of the emphasis on activities about which he had little or no knowledge: agriculture, livestock, carpentry, health care, and so on. As Rebecca Moore has pointed out, "The FBI has hundreds of tape recorded meetings which feature livestock and agriculture reports. Department leaders worked in relative freedom" (Moore 1985, 259). The more specialists were needed to run the daily operations of Jonestown—and this was certainly more the case in Guyana than in San Francisco— the less authority Jones had to make or influence decisions. In Guyana Jim Jones became more important symbolically as a mascot of cohesion than as a leader in the managerial sense. This shift had already taken place on a lesser scale as a result of the move from Indiana to California where people who were skilled at untangling the bureaucratic labyrinth of the social welfare system became more central to the Peoples Temple ministry. In Indiana Jones managed his church. In Guyana Jones was managed by his church.

There was a transition away from a focus on Jones at Jonestown in part because of a change in emphasis on the kind of healing taking place. As mentioned in chapter 5, Jim Jones's apparent ability to perform miraculous healings was one of the attractions for people who joined his sect during the Indiana days. Even in the early 1970s in California there was an attempt on the part of the inner circle to "help" Jones to perform these cures to attract people to the movement. What motivated Carolyn Layton and others in leadership to assist in staging these faked healings was the belief that the ends justified the means; that, although people might be initially attracted because of the healings, in the end they would stay in Peoples Temple because of a commitment to social justice and the apostolic socialism they were modeling for the world (Reiterman 1982, 158–59). Alongside the "divine" healings that could be provided by Jones alone, there had always been a commitment—embodied initially by Marceline Jones —to provide top quality orthodox medical care for the elderly people who were a central concern for the movement since its inception.

As Peoples Temple grew in numbers and political influence in San Francisco, this focus on standard medical care came to be emphasized over the miraculous healings of Jim Jones. The healing power decentralized within the group and made the leadership less dependent on Jim Jones himself for attracting new members or for keeping current members satisfied. Although many scholars have suggested that it was primarily Jones's paranoia and the inner circle's utopian ideology that drove the group to relocate to Guyana, I suggest that in addition to these reasons the move constituted a cost-effective measure to consolidate the care for the elderly and children who made up the majority of members of Peoples Temple. It cost less to provide medical care, housing, and a safe environment for the community in one location than it did to call on services spread throughout San Francisco, Los Angeles, Redwood Valley, and Ukiah. There is no indication that at Jonestown Jim Jones ever performed a divine healing. The medical care was provided by a staff of well-trained nurses and a doctor, Larry Schacht, who had been sent to medical school at Temple expense. It is ironic, in a way, that the agricultural mission in Guyana was named Jonestown as, significantly, Jones himself was less central to the religious organization than at any point before the move. One of the reasons for the marginalization of Jones's charismatic authority within his own movement was probably his increasing dependence on drugs and his subsequent lack of reliability. The most important shift that occurred when Peoples Temple moved to Jonestown was that Jim Jones became a liability rather than an asset to the community.

Jones's Deteriorating Mental and Physical Health

Many authors have raised the issue of Jones's drug abuse but, generally, by way of demonstrating his unique privileges relative to those of the average Peoples Temple member, who was forbidden the use of drugs. I suggest that his incapacitation from drug abuse shifted the responsibility for the community more and more into the hands of his inner circle. The most reliable evidence of Jones's drug dependence comes from the observations of his physician, the postmortem autopsy report, and the comments of his son, Stephan Jones. Rebecca Moore notes that Dr. Carlton Goodlett, Jones's physician in San Francisco, said that Jones was "frying his brain" with drugs and that he had noticed that the refrigerator in Jones's cabin at Jonestown was well stocked with drugs (Moore 1985, 221). The autopsy report on Jim Jones reveals that he had been ingesting pentobarbital, a tranquilizer, for a long-enough period before dying that his body had built up a resistance to its potentially lethal effects:

> The tissue levels of pentobarbital are within the toxic range, and in some cases of drug overdose, have been sufficient to cause death. The liver and kidney pentobarbital levels are within the generally accepted lethal range. The drug level within the brain is not within the generally accepted lethal range, and brain levels are the most important as far as vital functions are concerned. The cause of death is not thought to be pentobarbital intoxication because: (1) the brain level is low, as stated above (2) tolerance can be developed to barbiturates over a period of time and (3) the lethal level of a drug varies from individual to individual. (Moore 1985, 222)

Stephan Jones confirmed his father's growing incapacitation from abuse of drugs. He described his father as a "weak and sick human being" who was "pretty lost long before Jonestown." Jones was "whacked out on drugs" and often spoke both privately and over the loudspeaker in slurred words. His son believed that it was only a matter of time before the drugs Jones was taking would kill him. Stephan Jones observed that during the summer and fall of 1978 his father was "increasingly out of control" and would stagger about in front of Peoples Temple members, even urinating off the boardwalk in Jonestown within a few yards of where people were meeting (S. G. Jones interview, 7 Dec. 1992). Shiva Naipaul's interview with Andrea Walker, a

young black woman who had lived in Jonestown for six months starting in March 1978 supports Stephan Jones's observations. She told
Naipaul that she had enjoyed her experience at Jonestown until August 1978 when Jones started holding meetings every night: "He said
he wanted to keep everyone together. He was so sick he would talk to
us from his house with a loudspeaker. His voice was slurred" (Naipaul
1981, 153).

By 7 November 1978, only eleven days before the suicides, Jones
was "unable to walk without assistance . . . [and] appeared with his
face hidden behind a mask of white gauze" when consular officials
came for a visit (Naipaul 1981, 155).

Several observers commented on the decline of Jones's physical
health beginning at the end of 1977, when his mother, Lynetta Jones,
died, and linked it with his increasing abuse of drugs. Debbie Layton
Blakey, who had not seen Jones for several months before she and her
mother moved to Jonestown in December 1977, observed that Jones
had "deteriorated" since she had last seen him, that "physically, he
was a wreck."

> He had gained a great deal of weight, and he complained constantly
> of such a number of serious ailments that it was a wonder he was
> still on his feet at all. He claimed to have cancer, a heart condition,
> a fungus in his lungs, and a recurring fever of 105 degrees. He dosed
> himself with painkillers, tranquilizers, and amphetamines, which
> only added to the incoherence of his speech. (Yee and Layton et al.,
> 1981, 222–23).

The autopsy performed on Jones revealed that he, in fact, had
none of these ailments (Moore 1985, 222). Perhaps his claims of
serious illness were a way both to justify his abuse of drugs and to
explain why he was no longer as central to the life of the community.
Certainly, it was a mark of loyalty and commitment to give oneself
body and soul to the movement. Grace Stoen and Debbie Blakey both
mention that it was seen as a sign of one's commitment to the mission
of the Temple to have as little sleep as possible (G. S. Jones interview,
3 Dec. 1992).[2] Therefore, Jones's supposed ill health and subsequent
need for drugs was likely to have been perceived not as a sign of

---

2. See also the Blakey affidavit in Rose 1979, 170: "Dark circles under one's eyes
or extreme loss of weight were considered signs of loyalty."

weakness, but as a mark of the self-sacrificing leader who was willing to give everything for the ideas he believed in and the people he led.

At first his drug abuse appears to have been known only by a few —Marceline Jones, Stephan Jones, Carolyn Moore Layton, Annie Moore, Karen Layton—those who were the most intimate with Jones and, with the exception of Stephan Jones, helped him to acquire and take the drugs he needed. According to their passports, both Karen Layton and Carolyn Moore Layton made frequent trips to Venezuela. A private investigator indicated that Karen Layton's trips were primarily to purchase drugs for the Jonestown clinic (Moore 1985, 222). One FBI interviewee indicated that Carolyn Layton had made trips to Mexico to obtain illegal drugs to help supply Jones with medication for his various physical ailments.[3] Although there is no concrete evidence to support my speculation, could the initial decision to locate the Peoples Temple Agricultural Mission in Guyana have had more to do with the availability of drugs and the excuse to travel frequently to and from South America? Jones's publicly stated reasons were that Guyana was both safe in the event of a nuclear disaster and a socialist government.[4]

Marceline Jones and Annie Moore have each been identified by those who have written on Peoples Temple as involved in the management of Jones's drug consumption. What has not been noted is that each was in charge during two different periods of the Temple's history. Marceline Jones had been regulating and, in some cases administering, Jim Jones's drug intake since the Indiana years, when she used to inject Jones with vitamin B12 after his frequent collapses (Reiterman 1982, 74). Reiterman points out that it is not possible to know whether Jones was abusing drugs at that time but notes that he certainly had access to Darvon. "Whether he was abusing drugs at this time is not known—but he certainly had access to prescription drugs. He once

3. FBI, Guyana Evidence Index, 89-4286, report 19.

4. Upon what was the decision to move to California based? In casual conversations with residents of Redwood Valley during December 1992, several mentioned that the Ukiah area was "the drug capital of California," and, because of that reputation, they are used to people moving to their town to have easy access to drugs. Although the people I talked with had many negative things to say about their experience of having had Peoples Temple in Redwood Valley, many expressed surprise at how "clean" the members were with regard to drugs. The people of Redwood Valley are still very much affected by their involvement in the Jonestown saga and can recount people and incidents with great emotion and immediacy.

offered [Rev.] Winberg some Darvon for a headache" (583). By the
time they had moved to California Marceline Jones was attempting to
control Jim Jones's drug use. The following incident was said to have
taken place around 1970:

> He reportedly had begun abusing drugs, taking stimulants, painkill-
> ers and tranquilizers to suit his mood and purpose. Marceline became
> concerned about this new source of friction and psychological prob-
> lems. It came to a head once when she grabbed the stash from his
> medicine chest and, while Jones struggled with her, flushed his drugs
> down the toilet. (125)

It is not clear how early Jones's drug use became a serious problem
although the above suggests that it was earlier than the move to
Jonestown. A person who had moved with his family from Indiana to
California and was among those who defected in 1973 described Jones
as "probably being a heavy narcotics user" even at that time.[5]

In a sense the shift in power from the Indiana sect to the California new religious movement members is mirrored in the transfer of the
drug administering and controlling roles from Marceline Jones to
Annie Moore, sister of Carolyn Moore Layton.[6] Moore was the bond
nurse with access to the community's supply of drugs, a great conve-
nience in that it meant the amount and number of drugs Jones was
taking was not known to anyone but herself. In a letter written by
Moore to Jim Jones, which was discovered in Jones's cabin after the
suicides, it is clear that she had taken over the function that his own
wife had once fulfilled.

> I just wanted for you to know that I do not mind being your nurse
> and there is nothing more I would rather be. You should not feel
> guilty for having me watch you. I would rather be around you than
> anyone else in the world. I like to be here, it is not a burden. I will
> do everything I can think of to help keep you going. You have given
> everything to me so anything I can do for you is only right for me
> to do and I do not resent anything. If I seem irritated when trying

5. FBI, Guyana Evidence Index, 89-4286, report 2.
6. Although Stephan Jones does not believe that Annie Moore held much
actual decision-making authority at Jonestown, he believes that rank and file members
may have thought she did because of the access she had to Jim Jones (S. G. Jones
interview, 19 Dec. 1992).

to put you to sleep, it is because of frustration I have that it all has some bad side effect. But I am not mad at you. I will try not to show frustration any more. Sometimes I leave because I have to take care of other problems in the Bond or because I hope you will fall asleep before I come back but not because I don't want to be here. I like for you to be able to sleep and when they build the pool, I'll be out there checking also. I just thought I should let you know so you won't be feeling guilty about this. (I get more bookwork done down here anyway.) From Annie (signed). (Moore 1985, 306–7)

Apparently, some members of the community objected to the favored status that Moore enjoyed because of her position as Jones's nurse and Carolyn Layton's sister. In a letter written to Jim Jones at Jonestown Moore complains about a woman who was accusing her of behaving like an elitist:

Yesterday she had the nerve to say that Phyliss Chaikin preferred Terry Jones and myself being that Terry is Lew's wife and I am Carolyn's sister. . . . Then she was talking smart assy and said she knows Annie (me) takes Dad's blood pressure but she was tired of hearing about it (from me). Which I have only told her 3 or 4 times to my knowledge for why I had to temporarily leave work. I try to *never* tell her that that is what I am doing but Carolyn told me to just tell her one day that that was what I had to do. So I did and she used it. She said that I always had to go to East House [where Jones lived] . . . and that I just used Dad's name to go and goof off. (CHS, BB-2B-d-1)

By November 1978 it was becoming clear to those outside Jones's most intimate inner circle that Jones was on drugs. Ten days before Congressman Ryan's scheduled visit, two American Embassy officials paid a visit to Jonestown and reported that "Jim exhibited erratic behavior, slurred speech, and mental confusion." In addition Jones wore a surgical mask during lunch and "appeared to need help in standing up during a luncheon meeting" (Moore 1985, 307). Around that same time Jones's son, Jimmy, recalled that he, "found him [Jones] in bed and so doped up that he was nearly comatose. 'I dragged him into the shower, and stood there and held his dick so he could go pee. . . . He was passing green pee—always stuck with me, it was green-bean-green pee. He was telling me how Marceline was trying to poison him' " (Wright 1993, 81).

When I asked Dr. Chris Hatcher during our interview who knew that Jim Jones was deteriorating, he named Marceline Jones, Stephan Jones, Carolyn Moore Layton, Annie Moore, and Mike Prokes. Hatcher added that most of the membership probably also realized but that "they didn't want to know as much as they did" because to acknowledge to themselves that they were being led by a sick and drug-dependent man would be to call the commitment and sacrifices they had made into question (Hatcher interview, 1 Dec. 1992).

Cognitive Dissonance at Jonestown

This denial of facts to support an overarching worldview is an example of what the social psychologist Leon Festinger calls "cognitive dissonance" (Festinger 1957). According to Festinger, people's willingness to delude themselves about facts is in direct proportion to the degree of involvement that they have with the idea or group. A person will discount or avoid any information that might force a change in behavior or belief that has been held for a long time or has been committed to deeply. In short, it simply would have "cost" the average Peoples Temple member too much psychologically, not to mention socially and economically (especially in the case of urban black church members), to admit that Jones was anything other than the leader they had been attracted to and loved. The inner circle, by contrast, were faced with a sufficient number of "disconfirmatory facts" because of their frequent and intimate involvement with Jones to convince them that Jones had become a liability to the movement.

There are three possible responses to disconfirmatory evidence that challenge the group members' belief system: (1) discard the original belief; (2) tolerate the dissonance; or (3) underplay or discount the disconfirmatory event(s) (Festinger, Riecken, and Schachter 1956, chap. 1). The average residents at Jonestown could ignore Jones's drug abuse because their individual contact with him was limited and their experience of Peoples Temple depended more on the immediate circle of friends and fellow members with whom they lived and worked than on their personal relationship with Jones. The people who were in the most intimate contact with Jones, however, did not have that option. Their loyalty to Peoples Temple's vision for a just society made discarding their belief in Jim Jones as leader very difficult. At the same time, Jones's increasingly erratic behavior made the problem difficult to ignore. Those who were close to Jones found their ability to tolerate the dissonance that this conflict created repeatedly challenged by the demands of communal life and the pressure from Concerned Relatives. According to Festinger, when cognitive dissonance becomes intolerable, only the continual reaffirmation of the belief system on the part of supporting co-believers will keep that belief system in place (Festinger, Riecken, and Schachter 1956, chap. 8). The demonization of Tim and Grace Stoen, the Mertles, and Debbie Blakey helped the inner circle to affirm the choice they had made to stay loyal to Peoples Temple no matter how bad things became. But, tragically, this demonization of those who had left made discarding their original beliefs and leaving the community an impossibility, so that eventually only death provided a way to end the dissonance and to stay loyal to the belief system. (The idea that life could be more expendable than a belief system was a possibility Festinger never considered.)

By May 1978 Jim Jones's status in Peoples Temple had changed. When Reverend John and Barbara Moore visited their two daughters, Carolyn and Annie, at Jonestown that month, Reverend Moore observed that there was an "enormous contrast between the adulation of Jim which was a part of the affairs we attended at the church in S.F. and L.A. and the absence of this in Jonestown." He concluded that this shift resulted from "living more distant from criticism"—perhaps the accusations against Jones by the media and the Concerned Relatives had helped solidify his centrality in the movement in the United States—and "perhaps more important, the project speaks for itself" (Moore 1986, 237–38.) Moore was very impressed with the community at Jonestown, particularly the health care for the elderly and the spirit of cooperation and love that he and his wife witnessed.[7] He suggested that the success of the community, which had been built through the collective efforts of all, not merely through the charismatic leadership of Jones, had shifted the emphasis from Jones the person to Jonestown the community.

By fall 1978 the ability of the leadership circle to keep Jones from discrediting himself to the Jonestown community may have reached a crisis. As Stephan Jones pointed out, toward the end in Jonestown "everyone wanted to make the hold that Jim Jones had over them go

---

7. For the article the Moores wrote upon arriving home from their trip to Jonestown see Rose 1979, 161–63, app. 10.

away"; therefore it took only a small, but provable inconsistency on Jim Jones's part to convince people that the "whole structure was corrupt" (S. G. Jones interview, 11 Dec. 1992).

Even Tim Jones, an adopted son of Jim and Marceline and a deeply loyal follower, went so far as to imitate his father's slurred speech over the public address system one evening in the autumn of 1978. As Jones's surviving sons recalled: "People were agog: no one had ever mocked Father. Even more astonishing was the fact that nothing happened to Tim as a result. There was a sense of liberation—and also of uncertainty. People began to allow themselves to wonder what life in Jonestown would be like without Jones" (Wright 1993, 80).

Just before this incident, Tim Jones had caught his father in a lie. He had been told by Jim Jones that a young black woman, Shuwana Harris, had been begging sex from him. It was not until Tim intercepted a note from Harris to Jones saying that she did not want to have sex with Jones again that Tim realized that his father was capable of twisting the truth to manipulate people. Shortly thereafter, Harris was seen drugged and incoherent, a situation the Jones brothers interpreted as an attempt by Jones and others to keep Harris quiet and compliant. Thereafter, Tim Jones was skeptical of his father's leadership. These incidences of broken trust between Jim Jones and his most intimate circle were repeated over and over again in the final months at Jonestown, according to Stephan Jones (S. G. Jones interview, 7 Dec. 1992). Stephan had had a similar eye opening experience some months earlier when his father had claimed he was being shot at by someone in the jungle and sent Stephan out after the gunman. Stephan, who spent a great deal of time in the jungle surrounding Jonestown, knew that a person could not have approached from the direction designated by his father. After realizing that the threat to his father's life had been a fake, Stephan began to question his father's leadership more generally, and even vocally, in the community.

A useful theoretical method that Michel Foucault uses in his historical analyses is to go back to the time before the "rupture" in history that marks the shift from one paradigm to another and to examine the various possibilities still in play that later disappeared. "It is fruitful," Foucault has pointed out, for the intellectual "to describe that-which-is by making it appear as something that might not be" (Foucault 1988, 36). The importance of this method is that it screens out the "inevitability factor" that frames the outcome as having been the result of predictable and cumulative causes. The result of applying Foucault's method is that the shift that does take place or, as in the case of Jonestown, the decision that *does* get made is represented in the context of the complex dynamics that influenced it. The three possibilities other than suicide that the Jonestown leadership could have chosen were to (1) maintain the status quo, (2) disperse the community, or (3) replace Jim Jones as leader.

As suggested above, maintaining the status quo was increasingly difficult at Jonestown because of Jones's drug dependence and the mounting pressure from the lobbying efforts of Concerned Relatives. In addition, the relationship between Jonestown and the Guyanese government, which had been supporting the community for its own political reasons, had the potential to change because of the negative news coverage Peoples Temple was receiving and the involvement of a U.S. congressional representative in the investigation of Jonestown. But even more important was the plain fact that to continue Jonestown as it had been functioning for the previous twelve months would have meant a continuation of the exhaustion and pressure for the third of the community who worked to support the rest. Something had to change.

Reactions to the Increase in Internal Pressure

In his interviews with me Stephan Jones stressed that although the "aristocracy," or "white elite" as he sometimes called them, had more authority at Jonestown than did the majority of members, they did not have special privileges. They worked the same hours and ate the same food as everyone else. He called the women who surrounded his father "sacrificial martyrs," who were controlled by their desire to win Jones's approval and to prove to the rest of the community that they were as committed to the cause of social justice, although they were white, as any urban black person (S. G. Jones interview, 11 Dec. 1992). Further, by the time Debbie Blakey defected in May 1978, the leadership was constantly in turmoil, with frequent reactions of depression and anger to the predictable challenges of living in community (S. G. Jones interview, 19 Dec. 1992). Leading Jonestown was no longer any fun. It was constant work, and neither Jones nor the members of the community seemed to appreciate the long hours and dedication of the inner circle.

As tired and dispirited as they were, dispersing the community was not an option for the inner circle in part because of the consistent demonization of those who had left Peoples Temple. To give up would have been, in effect, to surrender to the demands of the Concerned Relatives and defectors such as Tim Stoen and Debbie Layton. By the fall of 1978 even to suggest such an option would have been seen by Jones and others in leadership as an act of treachery and betrayal. But if neither status quo nor dispersal were viable options, what of replacing Jones as leader of the movement?

Was a Peoples Temple without Jim Jones as charismatic leader ever a serious consideration for those in leadership? Aside from the shift explored earlier, which suggests that the group in Guyana was no longer dependent on him as a healer or manager and that his role as charismatic leader was no longer as central to the Temple because recruitment was no longer a primary concern, an exercise that took place in a security meeting might be interpreted as a "trial balloon" for replacing Jones. The question was, "What would be my reaction if you [Jones] were to suddenly be assassinated or die?" (It is not clear from the documents under what circumstances the question was asked or whether Jones was present.) The date on the answer by Mary Lou Clancey was 4 July 1978. She was a white female, twenty-four years of age, with just over one year of college education, and with training as a community health worker. She joined the Temple in Redwood Valley and would die, along with the others, at Jonestown. She was part of the Peoples Temple Planning Commission in San Francisco and served on the security council at Jonestown. After vowing "revenge" as her first priority, she wrote:

> The continuation of Jonestown would be the hard part. Because it has been *your* total commitment and strategies that have kept our organization going in a positive strain . . . I know myself that I could do my best to maintain under a new (designated by you) leadership —and continue to aid the work by following the princibles [sic] and guidelines you have so carefully & thoroughly set. If this would be the collective decision I would help. This may mean "putting under the gun" many so-called followers who could not maintain. *So be it.* (CHS, C-5-a-5/5a; italics in original)

The minutes of a Peoples Rally Agricultural Meeting (the "Peoples Rally," sometimes referred to as the "Peoples Forum," described in Peoples Temple literature as "the primary governing body including all citizens, practicing a total participatory democracy, even of school-age children" [CHS C-11-e-14b]) for that same day, July 4, state, "The new system of Troika was explained down thru all the individual departments" (C.H.S C-11-d-5a). Troika, or the Triumvirate, as it is sometimes referred to in other Jonestown reports, was never clearly spelled out in any of the documents. It appears to have been an expansion in leadership with an attempt to include two people, in addition to Jones, in the central leadership role at Jonestown.[8] Three days prior, on 1 July, at another Peoples Rally a note at the bottom of the agenda reads, "Reminder: Dad said publicly wants to discuss new management idea" (CHS, C-11-d-6). It is possible that Jones was cooperating with the coup because he was himself aware that fatigue and drug abuse were making him incapable of leading the community. On 5 July there was a meeting of the "Troika with the ACACs" (CHS, C-11a-17a). The ACACs were the members of the Community Advisory Committee at Jonestown, essentially the representatives of the community to the leadership circle.

From the information currently available it is not possible to know who would have run Jonestown had Jim Jones either died or otherwise stepped down from leadership. The FBI documents cited in chapter 4 suggest that Carolyn Layton was a possibility. Grace Stoen, when commenting on Mike Prokes's March 1979 suicide, suggests he was another possibility:

> I was very disappointed in Mike . . . because he has "off the record" told reporters he used to work with in Modesto that Jones was a bad person and that he did terrible things to his members. Mike wanted to leave, but the only reason he stayed in the church was because he was counting on Jones dying soon and he wanted to be there to help run the Jonestown commune correctly. (Naipaul 1981, 169)

It is possible that Carolyn Layton and Mike Prokes might have been leadership possibilities together as they were widely acknowledged as being among the "intelligentsia" of Jonestown (Moore 1985,

---

8. Reiterman (1982, 346) identifies the Triumvirate as Carolyn Layton, law student Harriet Tropp, and Johnny Brown Jones, an adopted son of Jim and Marceline; there is no footnote for this information, however, so it is difficult to verify.

100).[9] Hatcher has written that Prokes was "frequently called the number two person in the Jonestown organization," an assertion he based upon his many interviews with survivors of Jonestown (Hatcher 1989, 140).

Yet another potential leader was Stephan Jones, as suggested by an undated letter from Tish Leroy (a.k.a. Laetitia Eichler) to Stephan after a public conflict between him and his father. Leroy was a middle-aged white woman who had joined Peoples Temple in Redwood Valley. She had some college education and had been a Temple accountant and notary public since the early 1970s. She and her eighteen-year-old daughter both died at Jonestown.

> It was after you had contradicted and criticized dad, and then told the second in command to "fuck you," that I shouted at you. You were shaking the *fabric* of our organization and I did not think you realized it! The concrete walls had suddenly become cloth and looked *about* to rupture or tear. . . . You as a potential leader should have respect for the existing leader, *IF HE IS WORTHY!* . . . When you do not show it, then question arises [sic] that you in fact think him *worthy*. (CHS, C-10-a-c; emphases in original)

Not only does this suggest that replacing Jones was on the minds of people but it shows the precariousness of the leadership situation at Jonestown. What also becomes clear in the remainder of the letter is that while the community of Jonestown was being told that it was engaged in a total participatory democracy, in fact, the average citizen was a member of an audience being played to by the leadership. "Many times I have felt Dad did not have all the facts, or that he on occasion had not evaluated everything accurately—and I have written notes to this effect. . . . He has stated that we should NOT CRITICIZE HIM PUB-LICLY" (CHS, C-10-a-c; emphasis in original).

After discussing the plan to commit suicide and reaffirming her support of it, Tish Leroy closes the letter with a postscript: "Your Mom has my total respect & I'd not hesitate to follow her in life or to my death" (CHS, C-10-a-c). When I asked Stephan Jones what the dispute was about that prompted this public expression of his unhappi-

---

9. Carolyn Moore Layton and Mike Prokes were married in December 1974. There was, apparently, no conjugal relationship between them. The decision to marry was based upon wanting Layton's unborn child to be legitimate because Jim Jones, who was the acknowledged father, would continue to be legally married to Marceline.

ness with his father's leadership, he recalled that it was in reaction to Jim Jones accusing him of being afraid to die (S. G. Jones interview, 19 Dec. 1992).

This Peoples Rally at which Stephan Jones challenged his father, apparently included an unsuccessful attempt to solidify loyalty in the form of a suicide rehearsal. It took place sometime between when Debbie Layton Blakey defected in May 1978 and when her mother Lisa Layton died the following October. (Annie Moore writes about the Blakey defection and Dick Tropp's letter addresses some concerns of Lisa Layton.) Dick Tropp wrote a "personal" letter to "Dad" about the events of that summer night:

> I feel that it is my duty to share these thoughts with you. About an hour ago Lisa Layton said she wanted to speak with me. She said that after the white night she felt a kind of angry feeling inside. . . . She felt she'd "been had." Deceived. . . . She said she felt the information given to the congregation was inaccurate and incomplete, and that she couldn't make a decision based upon it. . . . I feel that Lisa's reaction is a danger sign. I personally did not know all of the details, but my feeling was very definite that we were being tested on our collective and individual determination to die. But this time, I felt that the kind of necessary collective testing didn't quite come across authentic. My apprehension is that among the Lisa Layton–Marlene Wheeler–Jann Gurvich segment of our community, in other words, people with a fair degree of savvy and intelligence, there is going to be a feeling from now on that the white night is really a kind of elaborate ritual testing . . . those voting against immediate "revolutionary suicide" are subject to questioning that contains within it a not-so-subtle intimidation that they are either cowards or disloyal or too attached to living. (CHS, N1C3a)

He closes with a reference to Stephan's public challenge and with a warning to Jones that continuing to test people's loyalty was having just the opposite effect from that intended: it was breeding distrust and anger toward Jones rather than building up the community as the previous white nights had. Dick Tropp's critique was taken seriously by Jones because he was among the educational elite at Jonestown, holding a master's degree from the University of California at Berkeley. Tropp, a Jew from New York and former professor of English at Santa Rosa Community College, was the author of most Temple press releases and was collecting material to write an authorized biography of

Jones when the suicides took place (Reiterman 1982, 428). He and his sister Harriet, a law student, were among the "aristocracy" at Jonestown. Apparently, his letter was circulated among the second tier leaders, for several letters within the files include comment upon it.

Around this time Tish Leroy wrote a private letter to Jones, stating her frustration with the way personal views were censored in supposedly "open" discussions about Temple policy.

> I observe a lot in silence, and though I can always justify the lies that get told, I deeply resent being told them—I understand the ends justify the means. The undersurface of me resents terribly being stifled and stopped in expressing—we are not allowed to give honest opinions, for these are dictated as policy and it is treasonous to have differing thoughts. Yet, I can also give you a whole list of "wrong" thoughts I did express, to the tune of being blasted and humiliated for it and told how wrong I was—only to watch events prove me right. . . . If we must "conform" our thoughts, I'll never make it. I must say yes with my mouth if it's good for the collective, but my mind will scream "no" till my dying breath. I feel at times like a misfit, but I know I'll never leave. I love what we have too much. It's far more important than me or mine. (Reiterman 1982, 430)[10]

An additional measure of the concerns that were foremost in the minds of the inner circle is the educational and self-analysis assignments that were given to members during the evening "adult education" classes. These written assignments on set questions were required for all adult members of the community. Two sheets of paper were to be handed in by adults, three sheets by high school students; they were part reeducation and part survey or poll. It is not clear whether these classes were weekly or more frequent or who designed them. Carolyn Layton may have been influential in the process because she was directing the Jonestown educational program and taught political philosophy. There is an emphasis in the questions on ideological concerns. Clearly, there was more than occasional rebellion against doing the assignments because the woman who collated the answers complained about papers not being turned in and teachers handing in incorrect lists of completed assignments (CHS, C-5-a-30). A random scan of the papers recovered from Jonestown after the suicides revealed the following topics: confessions of "crimes" against the community;

10. There is no note for this letter to indicate when precisely it was written.

why members had left the United States; to whom they were sexually attracted. Specific questions noted at the top of answer sheets included "how I feel about socialism and belief; the reasons that you brought us to this place of safety are; why I am here; self-analysis; methods to get enemies." The phrase "each according to his abilities, each according to his needs" was mentioned frequently in many of the answers, indicating that this was a central philosophy of the Jonestown community.

As one of these community assignments, Jonestown residents were asked to consider "Dad's worst pain." The most popular answers were about Jones's physical ailments and his emotional hardship as a result of "traitors" leaving the movement. Several answers mention Jones's "blood sugar problems" in particular, which may have been how Jones and the leadership explained to the community his drug abuse symptoms such as drowsiness and slurred speech. Certainly, Jones mentioned his blood sugar level with some frequency at Peoples Rallies (CHS, C-11-d-9c; C-11-d-11c; C-11-d-14a).

At a Peoples Rally on 20 December 1977 there is a note in the minutes that, "Dad collapsed due to the below 45 point sugar count. Dr. Schacht, Nurse Practitioner Parks and others helped to administer oxygen and medication to Dad" (CHS, C-11-d-14g). A considerable number of answers suggested that the reason for Jones's poor health was because of the drain that "selfish, inconsiderate, unkind and ignorant people" put on him (FF-5-n-8). Many people vowed to be better socialists and more loyal so as to spare "Dad" the pain of disappointment.

One answer to this question is particularly interesting with regard to the possibility of a leadership shift. "An extremely strong leader is needed to keep together this kind of group. Mother is the prototype of everything next in a woman . . . but I don't know if people are ready to follow a woman. Once you alluded to your concern about having a leader to follow you. I was thinking these thoughts at the time" (CHS, FF-5-m).

Another tantalizing piece of evidence that suggests a leadership transition was in the making comes from a letter dated 13 September 1978 from Jim Jones to his bank:

> It is my wish at this time that my name, James W. Jones be removed as signatory to the accounts I have established in your banking institution. Marceline Mae Jones shall remain as signatory to the above accounts. Further I wish to create a power of attorney over

these accounts in the name of Carolyn M. Layton. You already have her signature card on file at your bank. I wish this power of attorney to be the kind which survives after death. If there are any papers I need to sign in order to make this change please give them to Mrs. Layton to bring to me to sign. (CHS, A-40-c-4)

It is possible that Jim Jones knew how ill he had become and could see that his behavior was beginning to harm the movement to which he had given his life. There was, perhaps, a struggle within himself whether or not to step down voluntarily. Stephan Jones told several stories during interviews that demonstrate the level of stress and conflict within the inner circle during the fall of 1978 and their increasing dissatisfaction with Jones's leadership. These incidents are especially relevant because they take place among Jones, his two most intimate confidantes, Maria Katsaris and Carolyn Layton, and his son Stephan.[11]

In late September or October 1978, after yet another attempt by Grace and Tim Stoen to obtain legal custody of John Victor, Jones wanted Stephan Jones to help him stage a kidnapping of the little boy. Maria Katsaris provided most of the childcare for John Victor at Jonestown, and she objected to the kidnapping scheme on the grounds that the experience would be terrifying for the six year old. Katsaris told Stephan Jones that she would not allow him to go through with the kidnapping. This was a significant step for Katsaris to have taken because Stephan Jones had never before heard her question either publicly or privately a decision that Jim Jones had made (S. G. Jones interview, 11 Dec. 1992). In that moment Katsaris demonstrated a rupture in her loyalty to Jones, for she chose her love for John Victor over her willingness to follow Jones's orders.

The three scenes of conflict between Jones and Layton that Stephan Jones witnessed and participated in during the fall of 1978 were especially traumatic for him because during the ten years Stephan had known her, he had never heard Layton raise her voice or be visibly angry at his father until the ten weeks before the suicides. In the first

11. Katsaris was one of the young, educated, white women who had joined in the early 1970s. She had had three years of college and was twenty-five years old when she died at Jonestown. She was among the elite inner circle, and her father, Steve, was among the most vociferous opponents of the Temple and a central leader of Concerned Relatives.

incident Carolyn Layton called Stephan Jones to come to the house at Jonestown where Jim Jones lived with Layton, Katsaris, John Victor Stoen, and Kimo Prokes (the child of Layton and Jim Jones) because Jones was screaming at Layton in a Russian accent and accusing her of being a traitor. The Russian accent was not surprising as, according to a variety of sources, Jones believed himself to be the reincarnation of Lenin and would periodically stage "reincarnation" acts with a Russian accent. Reportedly, Carolyn Layton thought she was the reincarnation of Lenin's mistress. What was surprising to Jones was the level of hostility his father was directing toward Layton, screaming at her and accusing her of being a traitor, a counterrevolutionary, and one of the "Czar's minions." Layton was screaming back at Jones. Stephan Jones physically restrained his father until he calmed down. The second conflict occurred shortly thereafter when Jim Jones pointed a revolver at Stephan Jones and threatened to shoot him until Carolyn Layton talked him out of it. Finally, after the defection of Teri Buford in late October 1978, Jim Jones had a "heart attack," which Carolyn Layton, Stephan Jones, and everyone else intimate with Jones knew was a fake. Jones frequently fainted in the face of disloyalty or disagreement. When the family was summoned to Jones's bedside, Stephan Jones remembers looking closely at Layton and observing that she was "very upset, sullen, and stone-faced." While Jones was at his father's bedside, Jim Jones asked for an injection and told his sons it was "just B12." Stephan Jones remembers thinking that they had to "isolate him and get him off the drugs" (S. G. Jones interview 7 Dec. 1992. All three stories were told during the interview).

Layton's demeanor at Jones's bedside indicated her state of mind during the last months in Jonestown. According to Stephan Jones, she was "tired of living, worn out; she felt there was no hope and no future in Jonestown." Further, she was "tired of sharing the man she loved." Jones indicated that it was not only Layton who was unhappy with life at Jonestown, for there was widespread and deep depression among the white leadership during the fall of 1978. As Jones pointed out, "It was a weak place to be psychologically in order to change the world." By November decisions at Jonestown were no longer based on apostolic socialist ideology and the desire to build a model utopian society but on "appeasement and favoritism" (S. G. Jones interview 7 Dec. 1992). Those in leadership spent most of their time addressing the various internal and external crises.

Violence as a Reaction to the Increase
in Internal and External Pressure

Although Stephan Jones offers insight into the mindset of Layton
and others in positions of leadership, it is difficult to determine how
the rank and file members experienced the demands of life at Jonestown. One clue is provided by the answers to another of the exercises
given to the entire adult community. It queried, "What I would do if
there was a final white night." These answers, unlike many of the
others, were typed up by name onto a document that, I surmise,
was studied by the leadership circle. Willingness to die fighting for
Jonestown or by "revolutionary suicide" or by exacting revenge against
the "traitors" was affirmed over and over again by the writers. Of the
more than four hundred responses, which include answers from all
three "groups" within Peoples Temple, one, in particular, suggests that
there were discussions about what should happen to the children if
the Jonestown community was forcibly disbanded. Next to this entry
"please note" is typed in bold with stars around it. "I would like to just
drink some poison or what ever [sic]. I am still concerned about Billy
who doesn't say much and is scared to die. He is imature [sic]. If he
could be taken care of with the children I would feel free to go and
blow myself up with some tratiors [sic]" (CHS, C-5-a-23).

In another assignment—"responses to what one would do with
their body for revolution"—a woman with a four-year-old daughter
wrote, "This would be hard for me because I don't like to face the fact
of killing my own child" (CHS, C-5-a-33). By December 1977, when
Debbie Layton Blakey and her mother Lisa moved to Jonestown, suicide was openly spoken of at Peoples Rallies in response to any attempt
by the U.S. or Guyanese governments to remove children forcibly
from the community (CHS, C-11-d-11a). In response to a communi-
qué about delivering the Oliver children to Georgetown the 21 December 1977 minutes read, "Dad refused as always on the principle
that we would rather die." At this meeting Jones said that he wanted
"those who were afraid to die to be counseled" (CHS, C-11-d-11a).
Within five months the conditions at Jonestown and the relentless
talk of suicide would prove too much for Blakey, and she would return
to the United States, warning that Jim Jones and his followers were
planning mass suicide. In the wake of her allegations Jonestown residents were reminded, among the "do's and don'ts" when visitors came,
that "we don't believe in suicide" (CHS, C-11-d-1b).

The custody battle over John Victor Stoen became a focus of Jonestown security concerns and the issue around which talk of violence and suicide crystallized.[12] In August 1977 Grace Stoen was granted custody of her son by a California court. The residents of Jonestown responded by ripping up the summons served on Jones (Hall 1987, 217–18). A prolonged legal battle followed that was finally resolved only by John Victor's death on 18 November 1978. The significance of John Victor's custody grew as the perceived danger to the community at Jonestown increased. He became a representation of the community itself, not least because he was widely acknowledged as the child of Jones and was being raised as a future leader. Hall comments:

> For Peoples Temple, the issues involved politics and precedent. Whatever the claims to biological or legal paternity, John Stoen had been raised communally for more than half his life. . . . Like other communal groups, Peoples Temple altered the social claims of biological parenthood. The communal logic held that John Stoen's family was the group of people who raised him, and that he had a right to a destiny in the world where he was growing up. (1987, 222)

In an undated letter written "to whom it may concern" in the Guyanese government Carolyn Layton attempted to clarify the seriousness of the Stoen custody case.

> Pragmatically the issue of John Stoen is not an isolated custody case to us. From the political perspective we know that if we do not get backing on this issue, how could we ever have confidence in the government backing us on far more controversial issues. We also know that if John Stoen were taken from the collective, it would be number one in a series of similar attempts. It was indeed a precedent which if successful would give many others courage to make similar attempts. It was very much for the good of the collective that we decided as a group to make a stand on the John Stoen issue. (CHS X-3-b-2a/2b)

Later in the letter Layton indicates how far this stand might take Peoples Temple.

12. I explore the shift from protecting the children from custody claims to being willing to murder them rather than allow their return to the United States more fully in chapter 7.

One final factor to keep in mind was that a government official very high up told us when the John Stoen case first came up that we would just have to follow the process and that they could do nothing for us. He also said that Jim might just have to sacrifice John in the long run. This fact along with all the other events which followed added to our final resolve that we had to bring the case to the attention of all, and make a commitment on it, if the future security of the group was to be maintained. . . . *When we made our resolve we had no idea at all what the outcome would be, so we genuinely felt our resolve could easily end up in violence or death.* (CHS, X-3-b-2a/2b; italics added)

It is difficult to know if the black church members at Jonestown felt as strongly about the John Victor Stoen case as those who were closest to Jones or if their opinion about this or other central issues was taken into consideration. Stephan Jones stated that the Peoples Temple of California was different from the Peoples Temple of Jonestown and that this was especially apparent with regard to the status of black members. As Jones pointed out, "Blacks were second class in society, then made first class in Peoples Temple. When we moved to Jonestown, they became second class again." He said this was because the "white elite" who surrounded Jones were protective of their power and were unwilling to share it with the rank and file members who were mostly black (S. G. Jones interview, 11 Dec. 1992). In addition, a more complex racism was at work at Jonestown that relates to the connections between sex and power in Peoples Temple, specifically power linked to intimacy with Jim Jones. Jim Jones was uncomfortable with having sexual intimacy with black women because he believed in the "myths" about their sexuality. In the words of his son Jones was afraid of their "aggressive, almost animal-like sexual appetites." He was certain that he would be shown to be "sexually inadequate" if he had sex with the black women in Peoples Temple (S. G. Jones interview, 11 Dec. 1992).

Authors who have written on Peoples Temple have come to their own conclusions as to the reason why people went along with Jones in committing suicide. All agree that Jones was at the heart of the decision; their disagreements flow from different understandings about why the others went along with him. Rose argues that members of Peoples Temple were eventually compromised through Jones's combination of Herculean conscience and aggressive behavior. "He gave to people lacking a sense of inner authority a feeling that they were 'strong,' maybe even 'heroic.' He put them through 'tests'; he wanted to make them 'better people,' worthy of 'the cause' " (Rose 1979, 48).

A strong sense of heroism developed at Jonestown among the members based in part on the perceived (and actual) persecution by the Concerned Relatives and in part on the considerable accomplishment of having built a socialist community in the Guyanese jungle. This, in combination with Jones's increasing incapacitation, sowed the seeds for the shift to take place in which loyalty to Jones was left behind in favor of loyalty to the movement. As the reality of life at Jonestown became more painful, the community's significance as a symbol may have increased. Rose argues that "in the end, perhaps, Jones was partly or wholly stripped of the authority he had held so shakily. He had to rely on sheer power and substantial deception to carry out the final exercise" (Rose 1979, 46). Although I agree that Jones's authority had substantially unraveled by November 1978, it is only necessary to think that, therefore, "power and substantial deception" were necessary if one is wedded to the idea that Jones was by himself the final decision maker and most authoritative supporter of the decision to commit suicide.

Edgar Mills addresses the oft-asked question whether Peoples Temple had within its structure a propensity for violence. He has suggested that there is a variable in the potential for violence between sects and cults. He argues that the potential for "supercommitment, for unquestioning obedience" exists more strongly in cults because of an absence of a "natural damping process" that exists in sects because they are "rooted in longstanding traditions which themselves contain normative dissonance and serve to define norms and values that effectively damp tendencies to extreme behavior" (Levi 1982, 86). These "norms and values" may have amounted to a memory of what Peoples Temple had been in Indiana and how it had changed in moving to California and changed again in moving to Guyana. It is important to note, however, that this memory of what had been—this "normative dissonance"—only caused two family groups, the Parks and the Bogues, to leave with Congressman Ryan on 18 November 1978.

In spite of what Mills argues it must be pointed out that most of the sect members who were part of the Jonestown community chose to die with the cult and urban church members when "supercommitment" was asked of them. In the case of the Parks' and Bogues' families their commitment to one another as family units—perhaps solidified by the decision to move first to California and then to Guyana—

probably provided more of a "natural damping process" than any "norms and values" retained from their sectarian beginnings. There is also the problem, using Mills's analysis, in explaining why Debbie Layton Blakey and Teri Buford, certainly examples of more typical cult members, left rather than stayed to perform the final act of "unquestioning obedience." A careful reading of the transcript of the suicide meeting (see app. B) demonstrates that it would be more accurate to call what happened on 18 November "questioning" rather than "unquestioning" obedience. Christine Miller, an urban church member, challenged and questioned the decision that was being made yet, in the end, took the poison.

The fundamental error on the part of those who opposed Peoples Temple was to credit Jim Jones with all the power in the organization. Many accusations against Jones were made by the Concerned Relatives, mostly through the media, and a number of responses were written by Peoples Temple members in defense of their community. One, written by Jonestown resident Pam Moton in March 1978, was sent to both houses of Congress and closed dramatically with, "I can say without hesitation that we are devoted to a decision that it is better even to die than to be constantly harassed from one continent to the next" (Reiterman 1982, 409). This fueled a public protest by the Concerned Relatives, who capitalized on Moton's letter and accused the Temple of "human rights violations," including censored mail and armed guards that prevented freedom of access to the community (Hall 1987, 229). The Concerned Relatives believed that Jim Jones held all the power in Peoples Temple and that he needed to be forced through the courts or the U.S. government to relinquish control. They used the media in an attempt to sway public opinion in their direction. Their tactic was effective in eventually soliciting the involvement of Congressman Leo Ryan. Unfortunately, Tim Stoen and the others in opposition had failed to take into account the ways in which Jones's power and status had shifted since the relocation to Jonestown. As Rebecca Moore wrote with regard to her analysis of the public correspondence between the Concerned Relatives and Moton,

> The Relatives' error in the case of Pam Moton's letter revealed their assumption that Jim controlled every aspect of life in Jonestown and supervised every detail in the community. Our own experience with Peoples Temple before and after the move to Guyana suggests that Jim's authority actually declined in the jungle. John noticed on his

visit [in May 1978] that Jim-worship, while not eliminated, was not as pronounced as it had been in San Francisco. Carolyn's and Ann's letters from Guyana talked less of Jim and more of the work of the community. (Moore 1985, 257–58)

Could the tragedy have been avoided if Congressman Ryan had delayed his visit until after the first of the year? The evidence I have collected suggests that Jones would have either stepped down, been eased out, or died within several months. Had this occurred there might have been a mitigation of stress for the inner circle and an infusion of hope into the community as a whole. Probably, the number of residents at Jonestown would have decreased as those who were there only out of loyalty to Jones or who were unhappy with the new leadership left. Perhaps this relief would have led to less rigid boundaries between the people of Jonestown and their loved ones back in the States. But this is all conjecture, for Congressman Ryan did arrive at Jonestown with the Temple's two worst enemies in his entourage: the Concerned Relatives and the media. The result was murder and suicide.

7

Freedom and Loyalty, a Deadly Potion

*T*he questions of how the decision to commit suicide was made and by whom have not been frequently asked about Jonestown in part because of the assumption in both popular and scholarly literature that Jim Jones was primarily, if not exclusively, behind the decision. Therefore, asking why a sick, self-centered, possibly insane man would recommend a sick, self-centered, insane act to a community within his control, is a tautology. In this chapter I link the themes of the previous chapters with a consideration of the relationship between loyalty, betrayal, and the decision to commit suicide by the inner circle at Jonestown. I also explore the increasing hopelessness that contributed to the decision to commit suicide by the leadership circle and the motivations to end their lives for the Indiana sect, new religious movement members, and urban California black church members. I argue that each group, in its own way, was attempting to salvage a piece of the dream that had originally committed them to Peoples Temple.

Loyalty as a Central Community Value

The centrality of loyalty as a community value increased as threats to the unity of the group mounted by the Concerned Relatives, Congressman Leo Ryan, and the media gained momentum during the spring and summer of 1978. At the same time, a desire for freedom from the psychic stress and physical demands of life in a community where most of the population were dependent increasingly influenced the decisions of the people in leadership at Jonestown. Two women defected during the months before November 1978, Debbie Layton

Blakey and Teri Buford. These women were white, educated, and held positions of responsibility in Peoples Temple. These two defections were pivotal in the decision to commit suicide. Threats of community suicide by Jim Jones were generally tied to the defection of members as early as 1973, and this was the case with the final "White Night" as well.[1]

As discussed earlier, the desire to change the world and the attraction for Jim Jones as the embodiment of that enterprise became confused within the leadership of Peoples Temple: to love God's justice on earth was to love Jim Jones; to be loyal to socialist values was to be loyal to Jones. Any betrayal of Jones thus became a betrayal of the community and all that it stood for. Pam Bradshaw, who was one of the new religious movement members and was twenty-two at the time of her death, wrote in response to one of the Jonestown educational questions on "Dad's worst pain":

> I feel the most painful thing to dad is to see people who know and understand socialism, who have been highly trusted in the movement, turn back on all that is good and try to tear the cause down. Apathy, waste and unwillingness to change or to learn is painful and frustrating. Anarchy is another thing. Once when I had fucked up and gone out with Irvin, LC Davis and Michelle Wagner, I was telling Dad about it and he said, "Remember these people, it's people like them that are killing me." I do remember them and I also must carry my guilt for the pain I have caused him by my rebellion. I will not forget these people that have caused you pain. (CHS, FF-5-n-6/7)

In spite of this deep loyalty to Jones/Peoples Temple when the leaders' entwined loves for the movement and Jim Jones were brought into tension through Jones's behavior during the spring and summer of 1978, it was the movement that took precedence over Jones. Yet it was not the members of the movement who were a priority for these leaders. By November 1978 their loyalty was to the Jonestown com-

---

1. Although the term *White Night* has been used in most of the secondary literature as interchangeable with the *suicide drills* that preceded 18 November—so that the mass suicides are frequently referred to as the *final White Night*—it is clear from reading the California Historical Society documents that Peoples Temple actually used White Night to refer to any threat to the community, with revolutionary suicide being one among many options of response to that threat.

munity as a symbol and the power of the message it could send to America should it be unable to survive as a socialist community.

Weightman has suggested that "the members' relationship to [Jones] became so completely intertwined with their relationship to the church that the two became indistinguishable" (Weightman 1983, 136). Her statement is more appropriate as a description of the California Peoples Temple than of Jonestown. Because she does not take into account the shift that had taken place with the move to Jonestown, she wrongly concludes, "When Jones saw himself as having no way out, he saw there to be no way out for the Temple—and the members of the Temple agreed." Her schema of male agency, specifically Jones's agency, is carried over into her conclusion that it was Jones alone who was responsible for the suicides. The only responsibility the followers had was in agreeing with him. As suggested in chapter 6, the members themselves were more loyal to one another, to the ideals of the society they were creating, and to the leaders within their groups than they were to Jim Jones himself. It took Marceline Jones, Carolyn Layton, Maria Katsaris, Harriet Tropp, Jim McElvane, and the others in positions of responsibility and influence at Jonestown to embrace the idea of suicide for the rank and file members to have been willing to drink the poison. Jones had become too ravaged by drug addiction and paranoia to have planned the suicides on his own, or to have inspired people to take their lives through his encouragement alone.

If the leaders were convinced that they had failed at modeling how a socialist community should function, perhaps they began to see the importance of Jonestown as symbolic instead. In the unpublished "Response" to the accusations of the Concerned Relatives the anonymous writer admits that abuses had taken place, such as screening incoming mail, confiscating passports, and physical punishment (Moore 1985, 255). Reading through the various administrative documents from Jonestown that outline concerns about beetles, planting, clearing ground, diet, insecticides, livestock, labor organization, and so forth, it is clear that it required hard physical and organizational labor to create the utopian community that Jones and the leadership had imagined. It is no wonder that some people, such as Tim Stoen, Debbie Blakey, and Teri Buford, all of whom had the social and financial resources to return to mainstream society, decided to leave. The minutes of the Peoples Rallies and educational submissions by members reflect an increasing level of unhappiness and disappointment toward the end of 1977. This dissatisfaction was expressed in complaints about the food, the amount of work required, the number of meetings called, and the amount of time during the meetings devoted to disciplinary problems. The "Promised Land" was not proving to be paradise. As Chris Hatcher has pointed out: "The majority of Jonestown residents appear to have been aware of Jonestown's failure at economic self-sufficiency, the increasing failure of the medical clinic to handle tropical health problems, and Jim Jones' increasing obsession with external threats" (Hatcher 1989, 128). Perhaps, given these circumstances, the leaders began to wonder if the legacy of Peoples Temple would not be more positive if it were tragically concluded rather than slowly unraveled as a result of foundational financial, medical, and personality flaws.

Stephan Jones commented that his father gave many "orders," especially during the final months of Jonestown, which followers *knew* would be countermanded later. The community had learned to adapt to Jones's unpredictable behavior. For example, he related the story of how his father reacted when the summons was being served at Jonestown for Grace and Tim Stoen to obtain custody of John Victor in September 1977. Jim Jones gave the order that the guards, including Stephan, should "shoot to kill" anyone who came down the road to Jonestown. Stephan Jones understood, however, even at the time, that "everyone knew it was show." After some hours the order was changed from "shoot to kill" to "stop them." As Jones pointed out, this was the pattern of his father's leadership: an order would be given, then rescinded or modified. Members of Peoples Temple learned to overlook —or to interpret as a loyalty test—Jones's more histrionic statements (S. G. Jones interview, 11 Dec. 1992).

The question, therefore, is not, "Why did Jones order suicide?"— because the language of suicide and the practice for it had been going on since 1973—but "Why did the leaders choose to act on the suicide order at that time?" It is possible that the timing of the suicides had to do with a combination of the Ryan visit, which threatened the integrity of the community from the outside, and Jones's behavior, which was threatening to undermine the movement from the inside. If the destruction of the community was perceived as inevitable, perhaps the leadership decided to take advantage of Jones's remaining authority with the rank and file to make it a symbolic end, an end that would send a message to the world. For Jim Jones suicide may have been just another radical idea designed to test loyalty, a plan that he had always before countermanded. It is possible to speculate that as the dream of equality and freedom that Jonestown represented turned nightmare, the inner circle took Jones's talk of suicide seriously as a political and revolutionary tool that would allow Peoples Temple to succeed as a symbol where it had failed as a model.

A Consideration of the Link
Between Loyalty and Suicide

As mentioned, the threat of suicide within Peoples Temple and defections of members had always been linked. Jones first proposed suicide in response to the defection of eight young people in 1973. When this group of black and white youths left, they leveled charges of racism and elitism at the leadership. Jones responded by leading his inner circle in its first public exploration of mass suicide as a protest against (or, possibly, prevention of) group disintegration (Reiterman 1982, chap. 24). Starting in 1976, the first suicide drills were practiced among the ruling elite (Weightman 1983, 145; Wright 1993, 75; Chidester 1988, 31). At least one year before the suicides actually took place it was being discussed publicly at Jonestown and, according to Debbie Blakey, by March 1978 there were suicide drills involving the entire community.

> The only course of action open to us was a mass suicide for the glory of socialism. We were told we would be tortured by mercenaries if we were taken alive. Everyone, including the children, was told to line up. As we passed through the line, we were given a small glass of red liquid to drink. We were told that the liquid contained poison and that we would die within 45 minutes. When the time came when we should have dropped dead, Rev. Jones explained that the poison was not real and that we had just been through a loyalty test. He warned us that the time was not far off when it would become necessary for us to die by our own hands. (Hall 1987, 246)

The defection of the "Gang of Eight" in 1973 did not have any enduring negative impact on the Temple because none of the eight held positions of responsibility within the leadership (which was part of their complaint). In fact, Jones was so skillful at villainizing Jim Cobb and the others that it had the effect of solidifying group loyalty among the remaining members. (In fact, Jones stated [wrongly] that

Jim Cobb had been murdered to large applause from the Jonestown community at the suicide meeting; see app. B). The defections of Grace Stoen in July 1976 and Timothy Oliver Stoen in June 1977 had a more enduring impact both because they left huge managerial gaps and also because it taught that even the seemingly most loyal person could defect and damage the group. From the summer of 1977 throughout 1978, a period that coincided with the large-scale relocation to Jonestown, vigilance was constant against potential "traitors" among the leaders. A high degree of self-policing may also have been at work against one's own potential for disloyalty. The stress level within the inner circle must have been very high. By the time Debbie Layton Blakey defected in May 1978, with her subsequent accusations of suicide drills and sleep and food deprivation, the result was devastating. Teri Buford's defection in October 1978 may have been the act of disloyalty that set the wheels for the final White Night in motion.

Debbie Layton Blakey became involved in Peoples Temple through the influence of her brother, Larry Layton, and sister-in-law, Karen Layton. (Larry Layton married Karen, a Peoples Temple member, after his marriage with Carolyn Moore ended because of her involvement with Jim Jones.) When Blakey defected on 12 May 1978, she left behind her mother, Lisa—who would die of cancer in Georgetown during the summer—and her husband, Phil Blakey. Larry Layton was summoned to join the community at Jonestown shortly after his sister had defected. She and Teri Buford were central to the Peoples Temple organization, particularly its financial branch. "Control of banking and finances fell mainly on Carolyn Layton, because Stoen was occupied with other duties. Another staff member, Teri Buford, who knew mathematics but not finances, assisted her. And in late 1976 to early 1977, Jones added two other women to the financial circle—Maria Katsaris and Debbie Layton Blakey" (Reiterman 1982, 335).[2] Blakey became Maria Katsaris's assistant financial secretary. "As assistant financial secretary, Debbie Blakey knew the overseas banking system when she traveled from San Francisco to Guyana in December 1977. She was trusted and seemed to be tightly bound to the church" (403).

When Blakey defected on 12 May 1978, she was quoted as saying, "I'm leaving . . . I'm sorry. I know this comes as a shock to you, but I just can't take any more of this." She also wrote a letter to Jones:

2. Observe how, according to the ideological schema of the author in the passage just cited, Layton could not have earned her position by merit, but only by default.

"I have nothing vindictive against the church. . . . I'm just tired. I thought it was unfair to have a crisis when there wasn't one. People can't live on a string" (Reiterman 1982, 403). Blakey's departure was not only an emotional crisis for the community but also, potentially, a financial one. Immediately following her defection, Maria Katsaris and Teri Buford flew out of Guyana to change all the international bank accounts on which Blakey had been a signatory.

In a letter to Jim Jones after Debbie Blakey's defection Annie Moore wrote:

> I can't stand the thought of you being sick as I've seen you when "trusted" people left and did such sickening things. I could never stand the thought of being responsible for causing you added pain. I just couldn't do it. I have tried to imagine myself in with the sell-out traitors like Debbie and to self-analyze this aspect, but I can't really imagine it. I don't understand them. . . . I don't want to sell out no matter what. . . . I just want to do good so maybe some kind of change in the world will take place. (CHS, e-4).

Defections are the norm, not the exception, in new religious movements (Barker 1984, 146). Barker's data show that only 4 percent of the more than one thousand people she tracked were still full-time members of Unification Church after two years. The reasons for a person leaving a new religious movement include boredom, a need for less ideological certainty, a desire for more material possessions and more free time, anger over limited access to the charismatic leader, infighting with fellow members, homesickness, a decrease in the sense of purpose and exhilaration that attracted the person in the first place; all of these add up to the cost of membership being greater than the gain. A letter written by Debbie Blakey in 1980, reflecting on her experience, expresses a typical motivation for leaving an innovative religious organization that requires high commitment: she wanted a "normal" life. "Jim's growing insanity was one of the reasons for my defection, but another was that I wanted to settle down with a husband in a house of our own and raise a family" (Yee and Layton et al. 1981, 348). Hall indicates that there were many reasons why a person may have wanted to leave Jonestown.

> Some people became disgruntled early on, but not always for the reasons or with the intensity that the Concerned Relatives pro-

moted. Workers sometimes thought their skills were not used effec-tively. True believers lamented the decline of faith healings and religion, and they faced the disappointment of coming to terms with the less than perfect Jones as someone other than "god." Others found the work too demanding, or they longed for the light and life of the city. Whatever the complaints, Jonestown staff feared any dissatisfied person who left would be recruited by their opponents. (Hall 1987, 239)

A class dynamic is at work when predicting the likelihood of a person leaving any new religious movement and the pressure to do so by that person's relatives. It is notable that Concerned Relatives was made up of Peoples Temple family members who were overwhelmingly white and who were advocating for the defections of white, mostly educated, young people. Black urban church members were unlikely to defect, both because they did not have the financial resources and family support network to make that transition possible and because Peoples Temple, even during the more stressful Jonestown period, represented an improvement over their lives outside of the religious movement. For the California new religious movement members Peo-ples Temple represented a sacrifice that could be temporary. For urban church members Peoples Temple was an improvement in socioeco-nomic condition. There was little financial, social, or even familial incentive for leaving the group.

The affidavit that Blakey gave some five weeks after her defection, which is heavily influenced by the anticult movement ideology of the Concerned Relatives and has been widely quoted, is not nearly as insightful about what was going on in Jonestown in the spring of 1978 as is her sworn statement given at the American embassy on the day of her defection:

> I, Deborah Layton Blakey, hereby swear that the following statement is true and correct to the best of my ability. I have decided to leave the Peoples Temple Organization because I am afraid that Jim Jones will carry out his threats to force all members of the Organization in Guyana to commit suicide if a decision is made in Guyana by the court here to have John Stoen returned to his mother. *I know that plans have been made to carry out this mass suicide by poison that is presently at Jonestown. I also know that plans are made to kill the mem-bers who are unwilling to voluntarily commit suicide.* I believe that this plan will be carried out. I also believe that the Organization will

physically try to prevent any attempt to remove John Stoen from the custody of the Organization. In part for the above I have decided to leave the Peoples Temple. (Hall 1987, 244; italics added)

Debbie Layton Blakey's defection was pivotal in constructing an organizational dynamic within the inner circle that made suicide appear the only option. Blakey's departure must have been especially difficult and enticing for the women in leadership because she had been one of them and was similar to Carolyn Layton, Maria Katsaris, and Karen Layton in race, class, and family background. By committing the heresy of defection, Blakey left in her wake an insoluble puzzle. How could a person obtain freedom from the relentless demands of Jonestown *and* remain absolutely loyal to Peoples Temple? These two desires were, at their core, contradictory. Blakey's defection represented the freedom they desired, but her demonization showed the women the cost of this freedom. Loyalty to Jones had been compromised by his drug abuse. Loyalty to the movement was only possible insofar as the leaders were able to separate Jones from Jonestown. Suicide, then, became the action that would provide the ultimate in freedom and loyalty simultaneously. *Mass* suicide would make these deaths and the community at Jonestown symbolically significant.

An undated handwritten letter signed by Annie Moore and recovered from Jonestown after the tragedy outlines in detail the logic behind the decision to commit suicide:

I started out for revolutionary suicide, almost switched to fighting, but stick to suicide now. One main reason is that even though we have made arrangements for the children if we fight there is no guarantee that at that last hour to destruct, it would not be so late that the enemy would not be parading amongst our buildings searching for any one [sic] left and find us with few of our children dead. I would like to be on the front lines and fight, for my own personal decision but I would not do it without knowing the children were O.K. It is not my decision to make. I never thought people would line up to be killed but actually think a select group would have to kill the majority of the people secretly without the people knowing it. The way—I don't know. Poisoning food or water supply I heard of [sic]. Exhaust fumes in a closed area (carbon monoxide) I heard was effective while people are asleep. It would be terrorizing for some people if we were to have them all in a group and start chopping heads off or whatever—this is why it would have to be secretly.

People fight for their land and rights daily but it seems that if we did the same we would be categorized as the same—oppressed group struggling for liberty. If we killed ourselves maybe we would be categorized as lunatics but at least *we would be assured that our people could not sell out* or be tortured or taken and brainwashed (the children). The manuscript you mentioned could be sent to whomever—Russia or Cuba maybe even to the states though they would change it around. People would listen more to what we had to say because 800 people taking their lives would be quite something to read about.

They will lie on us no matter what we do anyway. If we fought it would look stupid if they changed the story that we were fascists fighting black Guyanese socialists because I believe the soldiers would be brainwashed against us—they wouldn't know who they were really fighting. From my experience in Georgetown—the Guyanese don't understand who we are anyway. I don't know what weapons we have but I think we don't have much of a chance of survival. We would be slaughtered. And then although I didn't think of it until someone mentioned it last night—they could probably add to their story that a lot of our people were cowards and ran away from them. Maybe Mike T. and Albert have a loyalty to this land since they have been here so long *but I think Americans grow up with no loyalty to anything—land or principle.* Many in the group have developed some loyalty—even new people since we have been here —*maybe they would fight to be true to you—which is why I would fight* —others to fight for the land. But what a farce it would be to be slaughtered and captured and risk our children's lives to be taken to the fascists. So I am staying here. I don't know how many would stand up to fight. *So I am basically cynical about how far you can trust our people. The main reason for suicide—to assure safety to the children and from the standpoint of history it would go down better and might stir others to become socialists or more active*—such a drastic action as suicide. It would be nice for our children to be able to grow somewhere communistically and safely but if this can't be accomplished I don't know. I don't relish the idea of participating in killing the children and I don't think anyone else does but I will do it because I think I could be as compassionate as the next person about it and I don't hate children. I know Stephan is true to you but some of the people who jump and say "fight" I don't think look at the consequences. It is an easy way out for some to just go to the front line fight and die and not have to be worried about the children or seniors or others injured or whatever who would no doubt be left to meet the fascists—*unless our planning was so secure as to assure death to the children and seniors*. At the point when I thought we should fight was when I was accepting that life will always fuck us over that our people would have to suffer—that's just the way life is—you will always get fucked over so what did it matter—our people deserved it anyway—why are we better than anyone that we can't be tortured also. *But then you said we could plan our deaths—we didn't have to just die—we could try to have impact on the world and save our children. So I switched back to suicide*. I felt like if we fought —maybe to each one it would mean something but it almost seemed to [indecipherable] well, we're going to get fucked over by life again, because I think there is *no* guarantee on our children dying securely in the middle of a battle. *With our plan now—the way we would like to do it—it may take up to two hours*. Also I think what a slap in the face to fascists it would be to take our own lives before they could have the pleasure of it. Then again they might probably be glad they didn't have manpower or guns to waste on us. They would have to clean up the remains and would have the story we had left to remember us by. I think life is a fuck over anyhow whatever we do but maybe less with the revolutionary suicide—so I stick to it. I'll do whatever is expected of me no matter what you have me to do.—From, (signed) Annie Moore. (CHS, EE-1-M-77–80; italics added)

The contradictory desires for freedom and loyalty are projected by Moore onto the entire Jonestown community. Constructing a scenario of mass suicide/murder was a way both to liberate the whole community and to keep them loyal. Annie Moore had learned the lesson of the Stoen defections: anyone could become a traitor. Because there is no date on this letter, it is not clear if it was written before or after the Blakey and Buford defections; however, my dating of it places it in the spring of 1978 sometime before Blakey defected. Blakey's sworn statement on the day of her defection indicates that the decision about using poison and murdering those who would not cooperate in suicide had already been made. It appears to me that Annie Moore's letter was part of the discussion that would have preceded such a decision. Certainly, suicide was discussed by the leadership more seriously as an act of protest after the defections of Blakey and Buford. Especially striking in the Moore letter is her reference to "saving the children" when she is actually writing about planning for their suicide/murder. Without access to this particular letter, which proves his point precisely, Chidester argues that at Jonestown killing the infants and children was understood to be a "redemptive act," an act that would save the children from being "brainwashed" into becoming the evil capitalist monsters who were the sworn enemies of Peoples Temple (Chidester 1991, 177–201). Death was preferable to disloyalty, according to the Peoples Temple ideology. Even the potential for disloyalty, which the children represented, was to be eradicated.[3]

Mike Prokes, who committed suicide in March 1979 after calling a press conference at which he read a statement in defense of the suicides at Jonestown, stated that, "Jonestown functioned on a high level of ethical behavior and human devotion you had to see and experience in order to comprehend" (Naipaul 1981, 149). Those who defected were mostly white people who were subsequently portrayed as being unwilling to make the sacrifices necessary to make a socialist community like Jonestown work. For Jones and the leaders there was no legitimate reason for leaving Peoples Temple. Naipaul interprets the loyalty of Prokes as indicative of a wider philosophy of sacrifice at work in Jonestown:

> The very rigors of their existence combined with the sense of external threat may have pushed them closer to each other. They who had given up everything to follow Jim Jones out to the jungles of Guyana might be brought close to despair; but despair does not inevitably lead to disloyalty. Revolutionary suicide would have made sense to many of them. (Naipaul 1981, 151)

The despair that Naipaul refers to was caused by the fact that only at great cost could one be disloyal. Thus, suicide was the only way to end the despair and to make the voluntary sacrifices of the new religious movement members appear significant to the wider world.

Teri Buford had been in Jonestown only six months when she decided to leave on 27 October 1978. She was one of the four women, along with Debbie Blakey (who had recently defected), Carolyn Layton, and Maria Katsaris, in charge of the international financial dealings of Peoples Temple. As Reiterman (1982, 463) points out, Buford "likely knew more about the complex Temple finances and bank accounts than anyone aside from Carolyn Layton." It had taken a great

---

3. Jones mentions at the suicide meeting that if the children are left, "we're going to have them butchered." See appendix B.

deal of disillusionment for Buford, who was one of the young white people who joined in the early California years, to act disloyally toward Jones and the Temple. Stephan Jones described her as one of the intellectuals, along with Carolyn Layton, Mike Prokes, and Harriet Tropp (a twenty-eight-year-old Jewish law student who ran the radio room at Jonestown), who developed the ideology of Peoples Temple (S. G. Jones interview, 19 Dec. 1992). Buford had been one of the hardest workers for the Temple throughout the mid-1970s. Her departure was a sure sign to the rest of the leadership—particularly Layton, Prokes, and Katsaris, with whom she had worked closely—that Jonestown had failed as a socialist community. She disguised her departure as an effort to infiltrate the Concerned Relatives (Hall 1987, 259), but, apparently, it was clear to Jones and the leadership at once that she was defecting. Buford was concerned, even in the end, that she not appear disloyal.

When asked in 1993 by the *New Yorker* reporter, Lawrence Wright, whether he would have taken the poison had he been there, Stephan Jones said that he was not sure.

> Loyalty to the community played a large part in the decision of the people to kill themselves, Stephan believes. . . . [He] had the opportunity to talk to two of the Temple members who had escaped into the jungle. "Everybody was under the impression that we"— the brothers—"were already out exacting revenge on the enemies of the Temple, and were giving our lives in the effort. . . . So it became a loyalty to us. . . . So there was a lot more involved than having Jim Jones standing in the pulpit saying, "O.K., we're going to die now." There was fatigue. I think everybody was defeated and tired. *They wanted relief from the constant emotional roller coaster my father put you through.* (Wright 1993, 88; italics added)

The Stoens, Blakey, and Buford were all new religious movement members whose defections hurt Peoples Temple organizationally as a whole, but who may not have had a great emotional impact on either the urban California black church members or the core group of Indiana sect members. Their symbolic importance for the rank and file members, however, was great. They became symbolic of the potential for disloyalty and treachery that lay dormant within each Peoples Temple member, especially within the white people, and that must be guarded against and repressed at all costs. Certainly, the group who chose to leave with Congressman Ryan, including two of the core families from Indiana, proved that point. The defections of the Parks and Bogue families may have been the event that caused Marceline Jones and the others from Indiana to give up finally in despair. At the same time, it may have illustrated to the urban black church members their superiority at Jonestown in at least this one matter: few of them had defected, and those who had had damaged the movement relatively little. This steadfastness may have contributed toward a perception on the part of the black members that their loyalty to Jones and Jonestown was irrevocable. In the end, when the poison was ready to be drunk, the black members may not have wanted to be accused of being like the disloyal and cowardly whites who had left.

The Defections on the Final Day

Sixteen people in addition to Larry Layton, who feigned defection in order to participate in the conspiracy to murder Congressman Ryan, left Jonestown with Ryan on 18 November 1978.[4] Scholars have generally numbered the defectors on the final day at fourteen or fifteen by omitting Chris O'Neill or Joyce Parks, or both (Reiterman 1982, 517–18; Hall 1987, 273–74; Moore 1985, 323–25; Chidester 1988, 153). Vernon Gosney, a twenty-five-year-old white male from California, and Monica Bagby, an eighteen-year-old black female, were the first to inform Ryan's delegation that they wanted to leave. Bagby's defection is scarcely surprising because she was sent to Jonestown against her will by her mother, an enthusiastic member, who wanted Peoples Temple to give her daughter a direction in life (Reiterman 1982, 473). She was the only black person to leave with Ryan on the final day. Gosney and Bagby were average members without leadership positions. Their defections, although painful for those who knew them well and, perhaps, damaging because they indicated to the media that some displeasure existed among residents, would not have had any discernible impact on the management of Jonestown. Nor, seemingly, would the departure of Gosney and Bagby have contributed to the sense of despair and desire for liberation already present in the lives of

4. The choice of Larry Layton as "trigger man" for the Ryan assassination demonstrates how central Debbie Blakey was in the thinking of those who orchestrated the final events. Larry Layton was not told to go to Guyana until after the people at Jonestown realized that Blakey had defected.

the Jonestown leadership. The decision to leave by the Parks and Bogue families, however, was a devastating blow for Jim and Marceline Jones and the leadership at Jonestown.

The relatively small number of people who chose to defect on 18 November and Jones's apparent overreaction to these defections have been used as further evidence of the instability of Jones's mind. How could a sane leader be unhappy with the departure of just a few when more than one thousand residents remained? The media was especially surprised by the events that followed these defections because they had been led to believe by the "concentration camp" propaganda of the Concerned Relatives that nearly the entire community would want to escape. Ironically, none of the people who left with Ryan that day were related to any of the Concerned Relatives. Journalist Charles Krause recalled: "It seemed to me that the Peoples Temple had a legitimate purpose, a noble purpose, and was more or less succeeding. The fact that 16 people, most of them members of two families, were homesick and leaving with Ryan didn't change that view" (Moore 1985, 325).

Even Peoples Temple lawyer Charles Garry, who knew the movement well, could not see any reason for Jones's reaction to the defections. "When 14 [sic] of his people decided to go out with Ryan, Jones went mad. He thought it was a repudiation of his work. I tried to tell him that 14 out of 1200 was damn good. But Jones was desolate" (Moore 1985, 324).

To understand the significance of the departure of the Parks group of eight and the Bogue group of six, one must place their defection in the context of the recent departures of Debbie Blakey and Teri Buford and the significance of the role, practical and symbolic, that these two families held at Jonestown. Both families held positions of responsibility and had dedicated their lives to the movement. Edith Parks was joined in defection by her son, Gerald, and his wife, Patty, their son, Dale, plus his wife, Joyce, and their two daughters, Tracy and Brenda, and Brenda's boyfriend, Chris O'Neill. The Parks family had been with Jim and Marceline Jones since the early days in Indiana, and at Jonestown they "practically ran the medical clinic" (Hall 1987, 274). Jim Bogue was the agricultural manager of Jonestown. His knowledge and expertise in farming had been centrally responsible for what agricultural success the community had known. His departure was cataclysmic for that reason but also because Bogue had been one of the original settlers of Jonestown and as such was seen as one of the founders of the settlement (194). Jim Bogue and his estranged wife, Edith Bogue, left Jonestown with their three children, Tommy, Teena, and Juanita, and Edith's partner, Harold Cordell. Few knew of their unhappiness because they had not been vocal about their dissatisfaction with life in Jonestown although they had been in communication with each other and had been planning to escape along with another couple (273). On the face of it, these were among the last people one would have expected to leave. Given their centrality, it is perhaps more understandable that Jones's reaction to their departure was to declare, "I have failed" and "all is lost" (273–74).

The Parks family may have been trying to negotiate a way to leave but not be disloyal, which would account for the fact that they had engaged in no public dissent. Even after the suicides, Edith Parks, the matriarch of the family, defended Jones's healing abilities as authentic, for she claimed to have been cured of cancer by him (Hall 1987, 21). Gerald Parks, Edith's son, when speaking to Judith Weightman about the move he and his son Dale's family made to Guyana, suggested that the Parks family had a special relationship with Marceline Jones that was as central to their involvement with the movement as was their relationship with Jim Jones.

> My son [Dale] who was in the church at the beginning had left. . . .
> He was a little more involved than we were. . . . He was in the
> medical field at the time, and still is. . . . And he was gone for about
> six months where he didn't even tell them, you know, where he was
> at. But they finally tracked him down. Marceline, Jim Jones' wife,
> talked him into going over, because they wanted him in their medi-
> cal area over there. . . . "If you'll go over," she said, "we'll give you a
> round trip ticket, just to go look at it; you can come back."
> (Weightman 1983, 87–88)

Later, when the decision came whether to have the rest of the family move to Guyana, Parks once again consulted with Marceline. "So we was gonna talk it over with Marceline Jones and two or three of the others, so we did sit down and I told her how I felt . . . and Marcie said—told me the same thing she'd told my son—she says, 'If you want to go back, you can go back.'" Stephan Jones indicated that Gerald Parks was in a position, because of his longterm relationship with Jim and Marceline Jones, to know "what was really going on." Jones believes that Parks may even have assisted in unloading the shipment of cyanide so knew that the talk of suicide had the potential of becoming action. He indicated that there had long been tension between Gerald Parks and Jim Jones because of Parks's loyalty to his family and love of sex. "He was not willing to totally subordinate himself to Jim Jones and Jonestown" (S. G. Jones interview, 11 Dec. 1992).

Certainly, the departure of the Parks and Bogue families was a blow to the Indiana sect. Importantly, the deaths of Lynetta Jones, Jim's mother and a founding member of the Indiana sect, Wings of Deliverance, in December 1977 and of Lisa Layton, mother of Larry and Debbie and mother-in-law of Carolyn and Karen, in summer 1978 may have been significant in that either one of them might have had the moral and popular authority to question the suicide decision. Neither of them are on record as having condoned such a plan. When Lynetta Jones passed away at Jonestown, the Indiana sect lost an important leader, and Marceline Jones lost an important supporter in her efforts to remind the founding Indiana group why they had chosen to follow the Jones family in the first place. Before 18 November it was primarily the new religious movement group who was filled with despair over the departure of significant members. With Ryan's visit, the Indiana sect experienced the same kind of central losses to its sector of the community. Had the Parks and Bogues *not* chosen to leave that day, it would have been difficult for the new religious movement leadership who had planned the suicides to convince the Indiana sect to participate. It took the added despair of such a great loss to make the sect members willing accomplices in their own murder.

When one listens to the audio tape made during the suicides, it is clear that Jones's primary hostility is toward the defecting members of Peoples Temple.[5] "The criminality of people. The cruelty of people. Who walked out of here today? See all those who walked out? Mostly white people. Mostly white people walked. I'm so grateful for the ones that didn't—those who knew who they are. I just know that there's no point—there's no point to this" (see app. B). An unidentified woman responds to Jones a few moments later: "Broke my heart completely. All of this year the white people had been with us, and they're

5. Substantial excerpts from the transcript of the forty-three-minute tape can be found in J. Z. Smith 1982, app. 2; also Rose 1979, app. 21. For a complete transcript of the audible portions of the tape see appendix B.

not a part of us. So we might as well end it now because I don't see
. . . [her voice becomes inaudible because of music and other voices]"
(see app. B).

As suggested earlier, the emphasis on the race of the defectors may
have built up the loyalty of the black members at this pivotal moment.
Stanley Hauerwas has recognized the racial implications of the defections. "People's Temple did become a place where blacks and whites
discovered they could be brothers [sic] once they had both discovered
who was their real enemy" (Levi 1982, 157). Thus, the defections
were a threat to the solidarity that had been built up in the community
by firmly identifying American capitalist society as the enemy. In
Jonestown, as in mainstream society, the whites held the power. It was
the whites who could choose life or death for the community through
their ability, socioeconomically, to defect.

The Suicides

Debbie Blakey claimed in her sworn statement given to United
States government officials on the day she left Jonestown in May 1978
that the poison was already at Jonestown. If true, this means that the
plan to use poison for mass suicide was already in place although the
actual decision had not yet been made. This suggests that the Annie
Moore letter quoted at length above was written before the acquisition
of the poison because the means of suicide/murder was still being
considered in the text of what she wrote. Perhaps the leadership was
gambling with regard to Jim Jones's health. Would he die before the
community fell to pieces? Was it possible to keep the community
together if he stepped down? Was revolutionary suicide the only way
to gain freedom and remain loyal?

Who prepared the actual brew of poison and calculated how much
would be necessary to kill more than nine hundred people in less than
two hours is not known. Without referencing her source, Weightman
suggests that Dr. Larry Schacht was responsible for the formula and
had calculated it "months before" (Weightman 1983, 63). Without
reference also, Hall declares that the liquid was prepared "according
to a recipe that already had been tested" and that the potassium
cyanide had arrived in Jonestown within the previous month, "perhaps
only four days earlier" (Hall 1987, 282). It is not known with absolute
certainty who distributed the poison. Based on interviews with people
who escaped into the jungle once the dying started, Kenneth Wooden

names Annie Moore and Joyce Touchette as the nurses in charge of the poison and adds that color-coded syringes were used for estimating dosage and magic markers for placing an X on people who had already taken the poison (Wooden 1981, 184). Reiterman mentions only Dr. Larry Schacht and "a dozen members of the Jonestown medical staff" (Reiterman 1982, 559). Hall writes that the potion was concocted and distributed by "Jones's aides and medical staff" but then adds that the "melange of tranquilizers and sedatives—Valium, Penegram, chloral hydrate—" which were mixed with the potassium cyanide, "came from the bonded pharmacy that had always been under the lock and key control of Annie Moore" (Hall 1987, 282). What is known for certain is that an unidentified woman's voice actually organized the people for taking the poison. It is a chilling moment in the tape of the suicides when her efficient and authoritative voice interrupts Jones's rambling speech:

> You have to move, and the people that are standing there in the aisles, go stand in the radio room yard. Everybody get behind the table and back this way, okay. There's nothing to worry about. Everybody keep calm and try and keep your children calm. And all those children that help, let the little children in and reassure them. They're not crying from pain. It's just a little bitter tasting. They're not crying out of any pain. (See app. B.)

Although Stephan Jones has chosen not to listen to the tape and so cannot verify the voice of the woman for certain, he speculates that it was Indiana-born Joyce Touchette because he was told by one of the people who escaped into the jungle that Larry Schacht and Joyce Touchette were involved in readying and distributing the poison. John Hall identifies the voice as Judy Ijames, Indiana sect member and nurse at Jonestown, based upon the testimony of eye witnesses (Hall 1987, 285). Whether it was Joyce Touchette or Judy Ijames, either one would have had authority both with the Indiana sect and the black church members: Joyce Touchette because she and her husband Charlie had been two of the original pioneers of Jonestown and Judy Ijames because she had provided health care for the elderly in the community.

When asked about the suicides and why he thinks they happened, Jones gave several reasons. He thinks that in the end his father was mentally unstable because of the drugs he was taking but that the

people around him "drove his [Jones] madness" with their "acquiescence to his bullshit" (S. G. Jones interview, 7 Dec. 1992). Because of
the pressure of the number of people living at Jonestown and the
amount of physical work it took to provide their daily needs, everyone
was tired, physically and emotionally, at Jonestown by November
1978, and the leadership was "depressed and disillusioned," particularly over the defections of the previous months (S. G. Jones interview,
19 Dec. 1992). The most important factor, according to Jones, was
loyalty. By the end this loyalty was not focused primarily on Jim Jones
but on specific beloved members of the movement. Nobody wanted to
let anyone else down by admitting that they were not committed to
the movement that had brought them together, even to the point of
suicide. There was also an element of coercion, Jones believes, although he was not there himself to witness it. Jim Jones had told
Marceline to call Stephan in Georgetown on 17 November after the
Jonestown basketball team had finished their match against the Guyanese National Team to tell him to return to Jonestown. Stephan
refused on the grounds that the team was "breaking barriers with the
Guyanese." The last words he said to his mother were, "You don't
have to talk for Dad" (S. G. Jones interview, 19 Dec. 1992). Jones
does not believe people were afraid they would be shot but were
afraid they would be thought traitorous by friends and the people
in leadership, particularly Jones. Although Concerned Relatives had
claimed that Jonestown was an "armed camp," the settlement actually
had only thirty weapons: ten pistols, thirteen small-caliber rifles, seven
shotguns and a flare gun (Hall 1987, 293). So the coercion was emotional and psychological rather than physical (S. G. Jones interview,
7 Dec. 1992). An element of "spiritual coercion" may also have been
at work as well. On several occasions Stephan Jones mentioned to me
that Mike Prokes and Tim Carter (both of whom survived 18 November because they were acting as financial emissaries) had told him that
the weather began behaving very strangely after Ryan's delegation left
Jonestown. The weather created the feeling of something "supernatu-
ral and ominous brewing" (S. G. Jones interview 19 Dec. 1992).

When I asked Jones what role he thought his mother might have
played in the suicides, he told me that Marceline "would never have
been involved in poisoning people, especially children." He pointed
out that the only person Jim Jones ever called "Mother" was Marceline; therefore, that part of the tape from the suicide meeting that
has generally been interpreted as Jones attempting to calm down

mothers generally is, in fact, Jones cautioning Marceline against re-
sisting what was about to happen (S. G. Jones interview 7 Dec. 1992).
"Mother, Mother, Mother, Mother, Mother, please. Mother, please,
please, please. Don't—don't do this. Don't do this. Lay down your life
with your child. But don't do this" (see app. B). Stephan Jones's
views notwithstanding, it seems apparent after listening to the suicide
meeting tape repeatedly that Jim Jones is speaking to the mothers of
the community broadly, not to Marceline Jones alone. Later in the
same conversation, Stephan Jones reluctantly suggested that if his
mother did participate in the suicides, it was "out of despair" (S. G.
Jones interview 19 Dec. 1992).[6]

There were two pivotal moments during the suicide meeting when
it was possible for people to see an alternative to suicide: one when
Jones was interrupted to organize the distribution of the cyanide-laced
punch, and one earlier in the meeting that was central in dissipating
any lingering doubts in the minds of the black church members. In an
extended conversation between Christine Miller and Jim Jones,
Miller, a sixty-year-old black woman, argues against the "arithmetic"
of allowing the defection of "twenty-odd" people to cost twelve hundred people their lives. Her public challenge of Jones and his responses
takes up the first half of the suicide meeting. She wonders why the
Temple can't relocate to Russia. She wonders how self-destruction
constitutes a victory over their enemies. Finally, in response to Jones's
insistence that there is no way to separate one person's fate in Peoples
Temple from another's, Miller claims, "We all have a right to our own
destiny as individuals. . . . And I think I have a right to choose mine,
and everybody else has a right to choose theirs" (see app. B). Jones
found it difficult to respond to this. Would Christine Miller's point
have carried the day had Jim McElvane not intervened? McElvane
was a black man who had arrived in Jonestown only two days earlier
(Hall 1987, 279). He was among a small group of blacks whose authority was respected throughout Peoples Temple. He had served as security chief during the California years and had not moved to Jonestown
with the rest because he was involved in running the stateside operation (Reiterman 1982, 322). McElvane spoke with authority and confidence when he responded to Miller (and the other silent members
who she, perhaps, represented) by saying: "Christine, you're only

6. For a suggestion about Marceline Jones's possible participation in the suicides
see app. B.

standing here because he was here in the first place. So I don't know what you're talking about, having an individual life. Your life has been extended to the day that you're standing there because of him" (see app. B).

Until McElvane "corrected" her Miller was still hoping that Peoples Temple could be the egalitarian, socialist community it was designed to be, whether in Russia or elsewhere. After McElvane spoke, there was a vociferous (although inaudible) argument between Miller and another woman. A few minutes later Miller attempts to say a few more words but is interrupted by Jones:

> MILLER: People get hostile when you try to . . .
>
> JONES: Oh, some people do—but—yes, some people do. Put it that way—I'm not hostile. You had to be honest but you've stayed, and if you wanted to run you'd have run with them 'cause anybody could've run today. What would anyone do? I know you're not a runner. And I—your life is precious to me. It's as precious as John's [John Victor Stoen]. And I don't—what I do I do with (*inaudible*) and justice and (*inaudible*). And I've weighed it against all evidence.
>
> MILLER: That's all I've got to say. (See app. B.)

Christine Miller's voice is never heard again on the tape. A few minutes later Jones announces that he has heard that Congressman Ryan and Patty Parks have been killed, and he becomes agitated and, later, incoherent. Then the voice of the unknown woman instructs the members how to organize themselves to commit suicide.

The voices of Jim McElvane and, finally, Christine Miller, concurring with the logic of sacrifice rather than dismemberment of the community they loved, represented the final step into the abyss. A bid for symbolic success designed by the new religious movement inner circle and agreed to out of despair by the Indiana sect was finally surrendered to by the black rank and file. What, after all, was more terrible to imagine, an end to life at Jonestown or the continuation of life back in urban America without their beloved community? In the end the members of Peoples Temple answered that question by drinking the potion.

8

Conclusion

Not everyone drank the deadly potion. Mike Prokes and the Carter brothers were sent with a suitcase of money to the Russian embassy in Georgetown. Maria Katsaris chose Tim and Mike Carter and Mike Prokes because they were Temple leaders and because Prokes had been to the embassy before (Moore 1985, 334). Several people, including black members Odell Rhodes, Stanley Clayton, and Grover Davis, escaped into the jungle. Peoples Temple lawyers Charles Garry and Mark Lane also fled before the dying began. Annie Moore and Jim Jones both died of gunshot wounds. The autopsy performed on Moore stated that the gunshot wound to her head indicated suicide was likely although there was also evidence that she had been injected (336). Before she took her own life, Moore wrote in her notebook, "I am 24 years of age right now and don't expect to live through the end of this book. I thought I should at least make some attempt to let the world know what Jim Jones is—OR WAS—all about." Her sister, Rebecca, speculates that because she used the past tense for Jonestown, she might have been writing as the suicides were taking place. Her "suicide note" for the community is a defense of Jim Jones, who she describes as "the most honest, loving, caring concerned person whom I ever met and knew." It is also a catalog of what the people had created at Jonestown:

> What a beautiful place this was. The children loved the jungle, learned about animals and plants. There were no cars to run over them; no child-molesters to molest them; nobody to hurt them. They were the freest, most intelligent children I have ever known. Seniors had dignity. They had whatever they wanted—a plot of

land for a garden. Seniors were treated with respect—something they never had in the United States. A rare few were sick, and when they were, they were given the best medical care.

In a different color ink at the bottom of the page Annie Moore wrote, "We died because you would not let us live in peace" (Moore 1985, 336–38).[1]

To put a human face on the horror of Jonestown and to hear the voices of those who died there it has been necessary to critique the ways the people, particularly the women in leadership, have been portrayed in the secondary literature. Crucial to this deconstruction has been the identification of ideological schemata that constrict and, sometimes, control the way scholars understand the behavior of women in new religious movements, in particular the acceptance of an unidirectional power flow from male charismatic leader to female follower and the uncritical linking of women and sex. I have suggested that the relationship among the women, power, and sex in Peoples Temple was more complex than the traditional sociological theories allow for. A restoration of the women in this scholarly analysis has helped to shed additional light on the events of 18 November 1978.

Peoples Temple was an intense organization that took itself very seriously. Previous accounts have not taken into consideration the role that the social complexity of the group might have played in the Jonestown tragedy nor how the intensity of the emotional entanglement of Jones and his movement might have contributed to the decision to commit suicide. It is an uncomfortable conclusion for me to draw, but a high degree of loyalty and a plurality of perspectives are probably difficult to maintain together in a community as demanding as Jonestown. Peoples Temple developed the level of loyalty that led them to suicide in part because its view of the world was based on a highly developed "insider-outsider ideology" and also because the views of only one group of people—the inner circle surrounding Jim Jones—were privileged over those of the others. Had the leaders of Peoples Temple been willing to say, "We've got one solution to the social problems of racism and ageism, but there may be others equally valid," I wonder how many of the educated elite would have been willing to move to Guyana? Perhaps part of the attraction for smart,

1. For the complete text of Moore's letter see Moore 1985, 336–38.

ambitious women such as Carolyn Layton, Harriet Tropp, and Teri Buford was that with Peoples Temple they got to be in the forefront of developing what they believed were *the* solutions to fundamental social ills. Being on the side of truth and justice for the disadvantaged had to have been a powerful motivation in their commitment; how much more so if they thought they were developing *the* model for solving the world's problems? The tragedy of Jonestown is that their pursuit of worthy Christian and humanitarian goals led them to destroy that which they valued most.

These women leaders found in Peoples Temple a structure through which to focus their considerable talent and energy. They did not have to spend the time that most do, deciding whether they were doing the right thing. One of the reasons the situation became so difficult for Layton and the others by the end was because the cognitive dissonance became so great that they had to start thinking through what they were doing and whether it was right. The most compelling letter in the Peoples Temple Archives was the one by Tish Leroy (Reiterman 1982, 430) quoted in chapter 6 in which she talks about the stress and pain of saying "yes" with her mouth and "no" with her heart. For years the new religious movement members had been asking, "How do we accomplish this task?" Suddenly, the situation at Jonestown required that they ask the far more complex question, "What direction should we go in?" and "Are we still on the right path, or have we lost our way?" The existing Temple theology and outlook did not allow for sophisticated, measured considerations such as these. Nor did it provide a way for the inner circle to get real advice from the sect and urban black church members. Because the edifice of egalitarian decision making had been in place for years—an edifice that gave the appearance of democracy but functioned more as a public forum for the "performance" of discussion—it was not possible for those in leadership to ask for the authentic help they needed to figure out the future of the Temple. To admit that Peoples Rallies and Forums were not truly democratic would have been too great an indictment of what had gone before. Peoples Temple was deeply invested in being in the right and was never very good at correcting itself or admitting its failings. By the end Jonestown was crushed by the debris of its self-righteousness.

This study has raised a number of questions about the role of heretics and traitors in the outcome of Peoples Temple. For the residents of Jonestown, especially those who were the most invested in the purity and righteousness of the Peoples Temple worldview, the traitor became the focus of what was feared most—an insider who is unmasked as an outsider, a person who appears to be a loyalist, but whose heart belongs to the "other." It is sadly ironic that this masked character—the heretic within a heretical movement—was such a central player in the tragedy of Jonestown as Jones himself had long been playing the traitor in Indiana and San Francisco. While Jones appeared to support mainstream liberal political efforts (and was rewarded for doing so), he and his movement were engaged in creating a revolutionary social order that called into question the policies of these same liberal politicians.

Could Jones even be called a traitor within his own movement? As the leader of Jonestown he was the ultimate insider, or so it would seem. As his drug addiction increased, however, his obsession with enemies, traitors, and death meant that his heart belonged not to the elderly black women or to the children who made up the majority of his community but to the "other." His energy was consistently poured into his confrontations with the Concerned Relatives and those who had defected. In the end, his nearly exclusive death by gunshot wound when his wife, Marceline, and his community died from poison, perhaps unmasks him as an outsider.

Carolyn Moore Layton, however, died as an insider. She loved both Jim Jones and Peoples Temple. For her, these loves were entangled with one another. In the end, she chose to die with her friends in the inner circle, not with Jim Jones. Perhaps, her last decision, where to die and with whom, reflects her choice of the movement over Jones. Perhaps, she died of disappointment. Maybe before she took the poison she realized that there could have been another way. I hope so. The last message Sandy Bradshaw received in San Francisco on 18 November was: "Hold on a minute. Carolyn wants to tell you something" (Moore 1985, 335). That "something" was never told. Layton died in Jim Jones's cabin, one-quarter mile from the pavilion, with thirteen other people.

> Someone had brought a thermos of cyanide. Another, a pan-full. The children, found in their bunks, were probably sleeping, or put to sleep, before being injected. A few adults drank the poison, while others chose injection. A few elected "double death": drinking and injection. They lay on their bunks, on Jim's bed, or on the floor, and went to sleep. (Moore 1985, 335)

Among the people who died in the cabin with Layton were Maria Katsaris, Jim McElvane, Layton's three-and one-half-year-old son Jim-Jon, John Victor Stoen, and Annie Moore (Moore 1985, 335).

A sign hanging above the pavilion at Jonestown, where the Peoples Temple community gathered for all their group activities, including the final one, quoted from George Santayana: "Those who cannot remember the past are condemned to repeat it." Yet, remembering, and the history that is written out of that remembering, is not an act devoid of political and social context. What is it that one remembers about Peoples Temple and Jonestown? Does one remember the mad leader and the brainwashed followers? Is one "remembering" anything that *actually* happened, anyone who *really* lived, when one does so?

The difference between foolish suicide victims and courageous martyrs may come down to what one remembers. Jonestown and Masada are separated not so much by the centuries as by the people who construct the memory of them. When one remembers a "brainwashed victim," one is both devaluing the person and the ideas and values that motivated the person. Was the tragedy of 18 November 1978 truly just a "cowardly defeatist act of final protest" as Tim Reiterman has suggested? (Reiterman 1982, 375). Or, is the *New Yorker* article, written with the cooperation of Jim Jones's three surviving sons, a more accurate reflection of the loss suffered on that day? "The great might-have-been of Jones's unlived future is whether he would have brought healing to the racially divided cities of America. It was that noble dream, however, which blinded Temple followers to obvious signs of internal decay, both in their pastor and in his movement" (Wright 1993, 74).

The legacy of Jim Jones is certainly one of grief and tragedy. Yet alongside this well-known tale is another story of Peoples Temple. One day, after I had been interviewing Stephan Jones, he left me alone in his living room while he went to change his clothes. I casually flipped through his wedding album and saw picture after picture of the most gorgeous integrated family. He and Kristi had been married only the year before, and their wedding party, made up of mostly family members, included black, white, Asian, and several children of interracial marriages. When he came back in the room, I mentioned how beautiful his family looked. His reply was: "Peoples Temple had a lot to do with that. Jim Jones had a lot to do with that."

My goal has been to challenge memories. If one remembers that which is comfortable, that which protects the status quo, is one not doomed to repeat history? Forgetting is a terrible thing. Remembering what never happened is, perhaps, more dangerous.

Appendixes
References
Index

APPENDIX A

Jonestown Demographics

TABLE 1. **Age at the Time of Death at Jonestown**

Age group	Age span	No.	Percentage (%)
Babies	5 and younger	70	8
Children	6–11	82	9
Youth	12–19	188	21
Young adults	20–35	229	25
Middle aged	36–50	89	10
Older adults	51–65	104	11
Seniors	66 and older	146	16

Source: "Personal Records—Members," MS3800 collection, Peoples Temple Archive, California Historical Society, San Francisco, California.

TABLE 2. **Work Experience and Professional Training at Jonestown**

Training	No.	Percentage (%)
Manual labor	117	13
Agricultural worker	23	2
Domestic worker	107	12
Secretarial	66	7
Health care	101	11
Management or professional	43	5
Underage or handicapped	291	32
Other	19	2
Unknown	146	16

Source: "Personal Records—Members," MS3800 collection, Peoples Temple Archive, California Historical Society, San Francisco, California.

TABLE 3. **Family Relations at Jonestown**

Family Status	No.	Percentage (%)
Single	302	61
Married childless or spouse absent	96	19
Small nuclear families	25	5
Large nuclear families	5	1
Small female-headed households [a]	50	10
Large female-headed households [b]	18	4

[a] One or two children per household.
[b] Three or more children per household.
Source: "Personal Records—Members," MS3800 collection, People's Temple Archive, California Historical Society, San Francisco, California.

TABLE 4. **Single Residents at Jonestown**

Age group	Age span	No.	Percentage (%)
Young adults	20–35	112	37
Middle aged	36–50	24	8
Older adults	51–65	57	19
Seniors	66 and older	109	36

Source: "Personal Records—Members," MS3800 collection, Peoples Temple Archive, California Historical Society, San Francisco, California.

Suicide Tape Transcript

JONES: How very much I've tried my best to give you a good life. But in spite of all of my trying a handful of our people, with their lies, have made our lives impossible. There's no way to detach ourselves from what's happened today.

Not only are we in a compound situation, not only are there those who have left and committed the betrayal of the century, some have stolen children from others, and they are in pursuit right now to kill them because they stole their children. And we are sitting here waiting on a powder keg.

I don't think it is what we want to do with our babies—I don't think that's what we had in mind to do with our babies. It is said by the greatest of prophets from time immemorial: "No man may take my life from me; I lay my life down." So to sit here and wait for the catastrophe that's going to happen on that airplane—it's going to be a catastrophe. It almost happened here. Almost happened when the congressman was nearly killed here. You can't steal people's children. You can't take off with people's children without expecting a violent reaction. And that's not so unfamiliar to us either—even if we were Judeo-Christian—if we weren't Communists. The world (*inaudible*) suffers violence, and the violent shall take it by force. If we can't live in peace, then let's die in peace. (*Applause.*)

We've been so betrayed. We have been so terribly betrayed. (*Music and singing*) But we've tried and as (*inaudible*) . . . if this only works one day it was worthwhile. (*Applause.*) Thank you.

Now what's going to happen here in a matter of a few minutes is that one of those people on that plane is going to shoot the pilot—I know that. I didn't plan it, but I know it's going to happen. They're gonna shoot that pilot and down comes that plane into the jungle. And we had better not have any of our children left when it's over because they'll parachute in here on us.

I'm going to be just as plain as I know how to tell you. I've never lied to you. I never have lied to you. I know that's what's gonna happen. That's what he intends to do, and he will do it. He'll do it.[1]

What's with being so bewildered with many, many pressures on my brain, seeing all these people behave so treasonous—there was too much for me to put together, but I now know what he was telling me. And it'll happen. If the plane gets in the air even.[2]

So my opinion is that you be kind to children and be kind to seniors and take the potion like they used to take in ancient Greece and step over quietly because we are not committing suicide; it's a revolutionary act. We can't go back; they won't leave us alone. They're now going back to tell more lies, which means more congressmen. And there's no way, no way we can survive.

Anybody. Anyone that has any dissenting opinion, please speak. Yes. (*Inaudible.*) You can have an opportunity, but if the children are left, we're going to have them butchered. We can make a strike, but we'll be striking against people that we don't want to strike against. What we'd like to get are the people that caused this stuff, and some, if some people here are prepared and know how to do that, to go in town and get Timothy Stoen, but there's no plane. There's no plane. You can't catch a plane in time.

He's responsible for it. He brought these people to us. He and Deanna Mertle.[3] The people in San Francisco will not—not be idle. Now, would they? They'll not take our death in vain you know. Yes, Christine.

CHRISTINE MILLER: Is it too late for Russia?[4]

---

1. Jones is referring to Larry Layton and the apparent plan to shoot the pilot of one of the airplanes that was to transport Ryan and his entourage, including the defectors, back to Georgetown from Port Kaituma. In fact, before the plane could take off, the men from Jonestown inside the tractor-trailer opened fire, and Layton never carried out the plan.

2. This line suggests that Jones was aware of the plan for the ambush at the airstrip. Perhaps Larry Layton was sent in case the trailer did not arrive in time, or maybe, Layton was sent as a "message" for his sister, Debbie Blakey, but his ability to carry out the murder(s) was enough in question that the gunmen in the trailer were sent as a backup plan. Given that Layton was not asked to come to Guyana until after his sister had defected, one wonders if he were sent for to participate in some activity (not necessarily this one) that would demonstrate to his sister and family that Larry Layton was more loyal to Peoples Temple than to his biological family.

3. Deanna Mertle, a.k.a. Jeannie Mills, along with her husband, Elmer, organized the Human Freedom Center after their defection from Peoples Temple in 1975 and were very active in the Concerned Relatives organization.

4. Miller was a sixty-year-old black woman who was born in Texas and who joined Peoples Temple out of Los Angeles. She had worked as a clerk before she moved to Jonestown and had some college education. She was among those "single residents" at Jonestown. See appendix A, table 4.

JONES: Here's why it's too late for Russia. They killed. They started to kill. That's why it makes it too late for Russia. Otherwise I'd say, yes, sir, you bet your life. But it's too late. I can't control these people. They're out there. They've gone with the guns. And it's too late. And once we kill anybody— at least that's what I've always—I've always put my lot with you. If one of my people do something, it's me.

And they say I don't have to take the blame for this, but I don't live that way. They said deliver up Ujara,[5] who tried to get the man back here. Ujara, whose mother's been lying on him and lying on him and trying to break up this family. And they've all agreed to kill us by any means necessary. Do you think I'm going to deliver them Ujara? Not on your life. No.

MAN 1: I know a way to find Stoen if it'll help us.

JONES: No. You're not going. You're not going. You're not going. I can't live that way. I cannot live that way. I've lived with—for all. I'll die for all. (*Applause*.) I've been living on hope for a long time, Christine, and I appreciate you've always been a very good agitator. I like agitation because you have to see two sides of one issue, two sides of a question.

But what those people are gonna get done once they get through will make our lives worse than hell. Will make us—will make the rest of us not accept it. When they get through lying. They posed so many lies between there and that truck that we are—we are done-in as far as any other alternative.

MILLER: Well, I say let's make an air-airlift to Russia. That's what I say. I don't think nothing is impossible if you believe it.

JONES: How are we going to do that? How are you going to airlift to Russia?

MILLER: Well, I thought they said if we got in an emergency, they gave you a code to let them know.

JONES: No they didn't. They gave us a code that they'd let us know on that issue; not us create an issue for them. They said that we—if they saw the country coming down they agreed to give us the code. You can check on that and see if it's on the code. Check with Russia to see if they'll take us in immediately, otherwise we die. I don't know what else you say to these people. But to me death is not—death is not a fearful thing. It's living that's cursed. (*Applause*.) I have never, never, never, never seen anything like this

5. Don Sly, the man who attacked Congressman Ryan with a knife, was known as "Ujara" within the Peoples Temple community.

before in my life. I've never seen people take the law and do—in their own hands and provoke us and try to purposely agitate mother of children. There is no need, Christine; it's not—it's just not worth living like this. Not worth living like this.

MILLER: I think that there were too few who left for twelve hundred people to give them their lives for those people that left.

JONES: Do you know how many left?

MILLER: Oh, twenty-odd. That's a small . . .

JONES: Twenty-odd, twenty-odd.

MILLER: Compared to what's here.

JONES: Twenty-odd. But what's gonna happen when they don't leave? I hope that they could leave. But what's gonna happen when they don't leave?

MILLER: You mean the people here?

JONES: Yeah. What's going to happen to us when they don't leave, when they get on the plane and the plane goes down?

MILLER: I don't think they'll go down.

JONES: You don't think they'll go down? I wish I would tell you you're right, but I'm right. There's one man there who blames, and rightfully so, Debbie Blakey for the murder—for the murder of his mother[6] and he'll—he'll stop that pilot by any means necessary. He'll do it. That plane'll come out of the air. There's no way you can fly a plane without a pilot.

MILLER: I wasn't speaking about that plane. I was speaking about a plane for us to go to Russia.

JONES: How . . . to Russia? You think Russia's gonna want—no, it's not

6. Jones is referring to the death of Lisa Layton, the mother of Debbie Blakey and Larry Layton. She had died of cancer the previous summer, several months after her daughter had left Jonestown. Jones is here asserting the idea that grief over her daughter's defection had hastened Lisa Layton's death and that her son, Larry, wanted revenge for it.

gonna, it's, it's, it's—you think Russia's gonna want us with all this stigma? We had some value, but now we don't have any value.

MILLER: Well, I don't see it like that. I mean, I feel like that—as long as there's life, there's hope. That's my faith.

JONES: Well—some—everybody dies. Some place that hope runs out because everybody dies. I haven't seen anybody yet didn't die. And I'd like to choose my own kind of death for a change. I'm tired of being tormented to hell, that's what I'm tired of. Tired of it. (*Applause.*)

I have twelve hundred people's lives in my hands, and I certainly don't want your life in my hands. I'm going to tell you, Christine, without me, life has no meaning. (*Applause.*) I'm the best thing you'll *ever* have.

I want, want, I have to pay—I'm standing with Ujara. I'm standing with those people. They are part of me. I could detach myself. I really could detach myself. No, no, no, no, no, no. I never detach myself from any of your troubles. I've always taken your troubles right on my shoulders. And I'm not going to change that now. It's too late. I've been running too long. Not going to change now. (*Applause.*)

Maybe the next time you'll get to go to Russia. The next time round.[7] This is—what I'm talking about now is the dispensation of judgment. This is a revolutionary—a revolutionary suicide council. I'm not talking about self —self-destruction. I'm talking about that we have no other road. I will take your call. We will put it to the Russians. And I can tell you the answer now because I am a prophet.[8] Call the Russians and tell them, and see if they'll take us.

MILLER: I said I'm not ready to die.

JONES: I don't think you are.

MILLER: But, ah, I look about at the babies and I think they deserve to live, you know?

JONES: I agree. But also they deserve much more; they deserve peace.

MILLER: We all came here for peace.

JONES: And we've—have we had it?

---

7. The belief in reincarnation was part of the Peoples Temple theology.

8. Jones is asserting his authority as charismatic leader in opposition to the logic of Christine Miller.

MILLER: No.

JONES: I tried to give it to you. I've laid down my life, practically. I've practically died every day to give you peace. And you still not have any peace. You look better than I've seen you in a long while, but it's still not the kind of peace that I want to give you. A person's a fool who continues to say that they're winning when you're losing. (*Inaudible.*) What? I didn't hear you ma'am. You'll have to speak up. Ma'am, you'll have to speak up.

WOMAN: (*Inaudible.*)

JONES: That's a sweet thought. Who said that? Come on up and speak it again, Honey. Say what you want to say about . . . (*inaudible*).[9] No plane is taking off. Suicide. Plenty have done it. Stoen has done it.[10] Somebody ought to live. Somebody . . . (*inaudible*) I'll talk to San Francisco—see that Stoen does not get by with this infamy—this infamy. He has done the thing we wanted to do. Have us destroyed.

MILLER: When you—when you—when we destroy ourselves, we're defeated. We let them, the enemies, defeat us.

JONES: Did you see—did you see, "I will fight no more forever?"

MILLER: Yes, I saw that.

JONES: Did you not have some sense of pride and victory in that man? Yet he would not subject himself to the will or whim of people who tell them they want to come in whenever they please and push into our house. Come when they please, take who they want to, talk to who they want to—does this not living? That's not living to me. That's not freedom. That's not the kind of freedom I sought.

MILLER: Well I think where they made their mistake is when they stopped to rest. If they had gone on they would've made it. But they stopped to rest.[11]

9. Jones's speech begins to sound slurred and garbled at this point.

10. Timothy Oliver Stoen represented the worst form of villainy and betrayal for Peoples Temple because he had been at the highest levels of the inner circle, had defected, and had been at the forefront of the efforts of Concerned Relatives to disband Jonestown. In essence, the community's "revolutionary suicide" was seen by Jones and the leadership as an act of murder by Stoen.

11. Miller is apparently referring to the people in the film Jones had just mentioned.

JIM MCELVANE: [12] Just hold on, (*inaudible*) would have made that day. We made a beautiful day, and let's make it a beautiful day. (*Applause.*)

JONES: We win when we go down. Tim Stoen has nobody else to hate. He has nobody else to hate. Then he'll destroy himself. I'm speaking here not as the administrator, I'm speaking as a prophet today.[13] I wouldn't (*inaudible*) talk so serious if I didn't know what I was talking about. Has anybody called back? The immense amount of damage that's going to be done, but I cannot separate myself from the pain of my people. You can't either, Christine, if you stop to think about it. You can't separate yourself. We've walked too long together.

MILLER: I know that. But I still think, as an individual, I have a right to—

JONES: You do, and I'm listening.

MILLER:—to say what I think, what I feel. And think we all have a right to our own destiny as individuals.

JONES: Right.

MILLER: And I think I have a right to choose mine, and everybody else has a right to choose theirs.

JONES: Mhm.

MILLER: You know?

JONES: Mhm. I'm not criticizing. . . . What's that? (*Inaudible woman's voice.*)

MILLER: Well, I think I still have a right to my own opinion.

12. Jim McElvane was a black man who had arrived in Jonestown only two days earlier; Hall 1987, 279. He was among a small group of blacks, including Rev. Archie Ijames, whose authority was respected throughout Peoples Temple. He had served as security chief during the California years. He had not moved to Jonestown with the rest because he was involved in running the stateside operation; Reiterman 1982, 322.

13. Jones is appealing to the role as prophet (charismatic leader) that he had fulfilled in California in an attempt to gain the authority to ask people to kill themselves. He is attempting to distance himself from his role as administrator (bureaucratic functionary) that he had increasingly shifted into at Jonestown.

JONES: I'm not taking it from you. I'm not taking it from you.

MCELVANE: Christine, you're only standing here because he was here in the first place. So I don't know what you're talking about, having an individual life. Your life has been extended to the day that you're standing there because of him.

JONES: I guess she has as much right to speak as anybody else, too. What did you say, Ruby? (*Inaudible.*) Well, you'll regret that this very day if you don't die. You'll regret it if you do, though you don't die. You'll regret it.

WOMAN 1: (*Inaudible.*) . . . You've saved so many people.

JONES: I've saved them. I saved them, but I made my example. I made my expression. I made my manifestation, and the world was ready, not ready for me. Paul said, "I was a man born out of due season." I've been born out of due season, just like all we are, and the best testimony we can make is to leave this goddamn world.[14] (*Applause.*)

WOMAN 1: You must prepare to die.

MILLER: I'm not talking to her. Will you let—would you let her or let me talk?

JONES: Keep talking.

MILLER: Would you make her sit down and let me talk while I'm on the floor or let her talk?

JONES: How can you tell the leader what to do if you live? I've listened to you. You asked me about Russia. I'm right now making a call to Russia. What more do you suggest? I'm listening to you. You've yet to give me one slight bit of encouragement. I just now instructed her to go there and do that. (*Voices.*)[15]

14. Jones has a strength of delivery in his speech, starting with his quote from St. Paul, not present previously.
15. Jones has exhibited impatience with Christine Miller for the first time. Unintelligible female voices in the background are arguing, probably the woman arguing with Miller and Miller herself. From this point on in the tape many inaudible, high-intensity, conversations are going on in the background.

MCELVANE: Alright now, everybody hold it. We didn't come—hold it. Hold it. Hold it. Hold it. Let law be maintained. (*Voices.*)

JONES: Lay down your burden. I'm gonna lay down my burden. Down by the riverside. Shall we lay them down here by the side of Guyana? What's the difference? No man didn't take our lives. Right now. They haven't taken them. But when they start parachuting out of the air, they'll shoot some of our innocent babies. I'm not lying—I don't wanna (*inaudible*). But they gotta shoot me to get through to some of these people. I'm not letting them take your child. Can you let them take you child?

VOICES: No, no, no, no.

WOMAN 2: Are we gonna die?

JONES: What's that?

WOMAN 2: You mean you want us to die . . .

JONES: I want to see (*voices shouting*) . . . please, please, please, please, please, please, please, please, please, please.

WOMAN 3: Are you saying that you think we could have smaller blame than other children were? Because if you're saying . . .

JONES: Do you think I'd put John's[16] life above others? If I put John's life above others, I wouldn't be standing with Ujara. I'd send John out, and he could go out on the driveway tonight.

WOMAN 3: Because he's young.

JONES: I know, but he's no different to me than any of these children here. He's just one of my children. I don't prefer one above another. I don't prefer him above Ujara. I can't do that; I can't separate myself from your actions or his actions. If you'd done something wrong, I'd stand with you. If they wanted to come and get you, they'd have to take me.

16. John Victor Stoen, the child in the midst of the custody battle between Jones and Tim and Grace Stoen.

MAN 2: We're all ready to go. If you tell us we have to give our lives now, we're ready—all the rest of the sisters and brothers are with me.[17]

JONES: Some months I've tried to keep this thing from happening. But I now see it's the will—it's the will of Sovereign Being that this happen to us. That we lay down our lives to protest against what's being done. That we lay down our lives to protest at what's being done. The criminality of people. The cruelty of people.

Who walked out of here today? See all those who walked out? Mostly white people. Mostly white people walked. I'm so grateful for the ones that didn't—those who knew who they are. I just know that there's no point—there's no point to this. We are born before our time. They won't accept us. And I don't think we should sit here and take any more time for our children to be endangered. Because if they come after our children, and we give them our children, then our children will suffer forever.

MILLER: Do you mind if I get up?

JONES: I have no quarrel with you coming up. I like you. I personally like you very much.

MILLER: People get hostile when you try to . . .

JONES: Oh, some people do—but—yes, some people do. Put it that way—I'm not hostile. You had to be honest, but you've stayed, and if you wanted to run, you'd have run with them 'cause anybody could've run today. What would anyone do? I know you're not a runner. And I—your life is precious to me. It's as precious as John's. And I don't—what I do I do with (*inaudible*) and justice and (*inaudible*). And I've weighed it against all evidence.

MILLER: That's all I've got to say.

JONES: What comes now folks? What comes now?

MAN 3: Everybody hold it. Sit down.

17. This man's statement, delivered with tears in his voice, changes the mood of the group. The next words of Jones are spoken with solemnity.

JONES: Say. Say. Say peace. Say Peace. Say Peace. Say Peace. What's come. Don't let—Take Dwyer on down to the east house. Take Dwyer.[18]

WOMAN 4: Everybody be quiet, please.

JONES: (*Inaudible*) . . . got some respect for our lives.

MCELVANE: That means sit down, sit down. Sit down.

JONES: They know. (*Groan.*) I tried so very, very hard.[19] They're trying over here to see what's going to happen (*inaudible*). Who is it? (*Voices*)

Get Dwyer out of here before something happens to him. Dwyer. I'm not talking about Ujara. I said Dwyer. Ain't nobody gonna take Ujara. I'm not lettin' em take Ujara. It's easy, it's easy . . . (*Inaudible.*)

Yes, my love.

WOMAN 5: At one time, I felt just like Christine herself. But after today I don't feel anything because the biggest majority of people that left here today for a fight, and I know it really hurt my heart because—

JONES: Broke your heart, didn't it?

WOMAN 5: Broke my heart completely. All of this year the white people had been with us, and they're not a part of us. So we might as well end it now because I don't see . . .

JONES: It's all over. The congressman has been murdered. (*Music and singing.*)

Well, it's all over, all over. What a legacy, what a legacy. What the Red Brigade doin' that once ever made any sense anyway? They invaded our privacy. They came into our home. They followed us six thousand miles away. Red Brigade showed them justice. The congressman's dead. (*Music only.*)

Please get us some medication. It's simple. It's simple. There's no convulsions with it. It's just simple. Just, please get it. Before it's too late. The GDF[20] will be here, I tell you. Get movin', get movin', get movin'.

18. Richard Dwyer worked for the U.S. embassy in Guyana and had accompanied Congressman Ryan's entourage to Jonestown earlier in the day. He had visited Jonestown several times before 18 November and was seen by the leaders of Peoples Temple as a supporter. Jones was interested in getting Dwyer out of the way so that he could not interfere with the suicides; nor could he be harmed.

19. Jones voice again is slurred.

20. Guyanese Defense Force.

WOMAN 6: Now. Do it now!

JONES: Don't be afraid to die. You'll see, there'll be a few people land out here. They'll torture some of our children here. They'll torture our people. They'll torture our seniors. We cannot have this.

Are you going to separate yourself from whoever shot the congressman? I don't know who shot him.

VOICES: No. No. No.

(*Music.*)

JONES: Let's make our peace. And those who had a right to go, and they had a right to—How many are dead? Aw, God Almighty, God. Huh? Patty Parks is dead?

WOMAN 7: Some of the others who endure long enough in a safe place could write about the goodness of Jim Jones.

JONES: I don't know how in the world they're ever going to write about us. It's just too late. It's too late. The congressman's dead. The congressman lays dead. Many of our traitors are dead. They're all layin' out there dead. (*Inaudible.*)

I didn't, but my people did. My people did. They're my people, and they've been provoked too much. They've been provoked too much. What's happened here's been since Tuesday's been an act of provocation.

WOMAN 8: What about Ted? If there's any way it's possible to, eh, have and to give Ted something to take then, I'm satisfied, okay?²¹

JONES: Okay.

WOMAN 8: I said, if there's anyway you can do before I have to give Ted something, so he won't have to let him go through okay, and I'm satisfied.

JONES: That's fine. Okay, yes. Yes. Yes.

WOMAN 9: Thank you for everything. You are the only. You are the only. And I appreciate you. (*Applause.*)

21. This is a young woman obviously talking about her son.

JONES: Please, can we hasten? Can we hasten with that medication? You don't know what you've done. I tried. (*Applause, music, singing.*)

They saw it happen and ran into the bush and dropped the machine guns. I never in my life.[22] But not any more. But we've got to move. Are you gonna get that medication here? You've got to move. Marceline,[23] about forty minutes.

JUDY IJAMES OR JOYCE TOUCHETTE:[24] You have to move, and the people that are standing there in the aisles, go stand in the radio room yard.[25] Everybody get behind the table and back this way, okay. There's nothing to worry about. Everybody keep calm and try and keep your children calm. And all those children that help, let the little children in and reassure them. They're not crying from pain. It's just a little bitter tasting. They're not crying out of any pain. Annie Miguel, can I please see you back . . .

MCELVANE: . . . Things I used to do before I came here. So let me tell you about it. It might make a lot of you feel a little more comfortable. Sit down and be quiet, please.

One of the things I used to do—I used to be a therapist. And the kind of therapy that I did had to do with reincarnations in past life situations. And every time anybody had the experience of going into a past life, I was fortunate enough through Father to be able to let them experience it all the way through their death, so to speak. And everybody was so happy when they made that step to the other side.

JONES: (*Inaudible.*) It's the only way to step. That choice is not ours now. It's out of our hands. (*Children crying in the background.*)

22. Jones sounds incoherent.

23. I am not 100 percent certain that Jones addresses Marceline here, but that's the most likely interpretation of the word. There is a pause just before he says this answer. I suspect that she had just asked him how long the whole process would take, and his answer was "about forty minutes."

24. See chapter 7 for discussion about the identity of the woman who speaks at this point.

25. In my view, there were two pivotal moments during the suicide meeting when events could have turned another direction had people with authority not spoken in support of Jones and the decision to commit suicide. The first was when Jim McElvane intervened with Christine Miller (see above) and the other is here when Judy Ijames or Joyce Touchette organizes the process for committing suicide. Jones's speech right before her instructions is slurred, and he sounds incoherent. These instructions focused the mood of the gathering. The suicides began just moments later.

MCELVANE: If we have a body that's been crippled, suddenly you have the kind of body that you want to have.

JONES: A little rest, a little rest.

MCELVANE: It feels good. It never felt so good. Now, may I tell you. You've never felt so good as how that feels.

JONES: And I do hope that (*inaudible*) will stay where they belong and don't come up here.

What is it? What is it? They what? Alright, it's hard but only at first—only at first is it hard. Hard only at first. Living—you're looking at death and it looks—living is much, much more difficult. Raising up every morning and not knowing what's going to be the night's bringing. It's much more difficult. It's much more difficult. (*Crying and talking.*)

WOMAN 10: I just want to say something for everyone that I see that is standing around or crying. This is nothing to cry about. This is something we could all rejoice about. We could be happy about this. They always told us that we could cry when you're coming into this world. So we're leaving it, and we're leaving it peaceful. I think we should be happy about this. I was just thinking about Jim Jones. He just has suffered and suffered and suffered. We have the honor guard, and we don't even have a chance to . . . (*Inaudible.*) I want to give him one more chance. (*Inaudible.*) That's few that's gone. There's many more here. (*Inaudible.*) That's not all of us. That's not all yet. That's just a few that have died. I tried to get to the one that—there's a kid (*inaudible*) I'm looking at so many people crying. I wish you would not cry. And just thank Father. (*Inaudible.*) . . . (*sustained applause.*) I've been here about one year and nine months. And I never felt better in my life. Not in San Francisco. But until I came to Jonestown. I had a very good life. I had a beautiful life. I don't see nothing that I could be sorry about. We should be happy. At least I am. (*Inaudible.*) (*Applause, music.*)

WOMAN 11: . . . Good to be alive today. I just like to thank Dad cause he was the only one that stood up for me when I needed him. And thank you, Dad.

WOMAN 12: I'm glad you're my brothers and sisters, and I'm glad to be here. Okay.

(*Voices.*)

JONES: [26] Please. For God's sake, let's get on with it. We've lived—we've lived as no other people lived and loved. We've had as much of this world as you're gonna get. Let's just be done with it. Let's be done with the agony of it. (*Applause.*)

It's far, far harder to have to walk through every day, die slowly—and from the time you're a child 'til the time you get gray, you're dying.

Dishonest, and I'm sure that they'll—they'll pay for it. They'll pay for it. This is a revolutionary suicide. This is not a self-destructive suicide. So they'll pay for this. They brought this upon us. And they'll pay for that. I leave that destiny to them.

(*Voices.*)

Who wants to go with their child has a right to go with their child. I think it's humane. I want to go—I want to see you go, though. They can take me and do what they want—whatever they want to do. I want to see you go. I don't want to see you go through this hell no more. No more. No more. No more.

We're trying. If everybody will relax. The best thing you do to relax, and you will have no problem. You'll have no problem with this thing if you just relax.

MAN 4: . . . A great deal because it's Jim Jones. And the way the children are laying there now. I'd rather see them lay like that than to see them have to die like the Jews did, which was pitiful anyhow. And I just like to thank Dad for giving us life and also death. And I appreciate the fact of the way our children are going. Because, like Dad said, when they come in, what they're gonna do to our children—they're gonna massacre our children. And also the ones that they take capture, they're gonna just let them grow up and be dummies like they want them to be. And not grow up to be a person like the one and only Jim Jones. So I'd like to thank Dad for the opportunity for letting Jonestown be not what it could be, but what Jonestown is. Thank you, Dad. (*Applause.*)

JONES: It's not to be afeared. It is not to be feared. It is a friend. It's a friend . . . sitting there, show your love for one another. Let's get gone. Let's get gone. Let's get gone. (*Children crying.*) We had nothing we could do. We can't—we can't separate ourselves from our own people. For twenty years laying in some old rotten nursing home. (*Music.*) Taking us through all these anguish years. They took us and put us in chains and that's nothing. This business—that business—there's no comparison to that, to this.

They've robbed us of our land, and they've taken us and driven us and

26. Jones speaks here and later with renewed energy and clarity.

we tried to find ourselves. We tried to find a new beginning. But it's too late. You can't separate yourself from your brother and your sister. No way I'm going to do it. I refuse. I don't know who fired the shot. I don't know who killed the congressman. But as far as I am concerned, I killed him. You understand what I'm saying? I killed him. He had no business coming. I told him not to come.

WOMAN 13: Right, right.

(*Music and crying.*)

JONES: I, with respect, die with a degree of dignity. Lay down your life with dignity. Don't lay down with tears and agony. There's nothing to death. It's like Mac²⁷ said, it's just stepping over to another plane. Don't be this way. Stop this hysterics. This is not the way for people who are Socialists or Communists to die. No way for us to die. We must die with some dignity. We must die with some dignity. We will have no choice. Now we have some choice. Do you think they're gonna allow this to be done—allow us to get by with this? You must be insane.

Look children, it's just something to put you to rest. Oh, God. (*Children crying.*)

Mother, Mother, Mother, Mother, Mother, please. Mother, please, please, please. Don't—don't do this. Don't do this. Lay down your life with your child. But don't do this.

WOMAN 14: We're doing all of this for you.

JONES: Free at last. Keep—keep your emotions down. Keep your emotions down. Children, it will not hurt. If you'd be—if you'll be quiet. If you'll be quiet.

(*Music and crying.*)

It's never been done before, you say. It's been done by every tribe in history. Every tribe facing annihilation. All the Indians of the Amazon are doing it right now. They refuse to bring any babies into the world. They kill every child that comes into the world. Because they don't want to live in this kind of a world.

So be patient. Be patient. Death is—I tell you, I don't care how many screams you hear. I don't care how many anguished cries. Death is a million times preferable to ten more days of this life. If you knew what was ahead of you—if you knew what was ahead of you, you'd be glad to be stepping over tonight.

27. Jim McElvane.

Death, death, death is common to people. And the Eskimos, they take death in their stride. Let's be digni—let's be dignified. If you quit tell them they're dying—if you adults would stop some of this nonsense. Adults, adults, adults. I call on you to stop this nonsense. I call on you to quit exciting your children when all they're doing is going to a quiet rest. I call on you to stop this now if you have any respect at all. Are we black, proud, and Socialist, or what are we? Now stop this nonsense. Don't carry this on anymore. You're exciting your children.

No, no sorrow—that it's all over. I'm glad it's over. Hurry, hurry my children. Hurry. All I think (*inaudible*) from the hands of the enemy. Hurry, my children. Hurry. There are seniors out here that I'm concerned about. Hurry. I don't want to leave my seniors to this mess. Only quickly, quickly, quickly, quickly, quickly. . . . Good knowing you.

No more pain now. No more pain, I said (*inaudible*). No more pain. Jim Cobb[28] is laying on the airfield dead at this moment. (*Applause.*) Remember the Oliver woman said she—she'd come over and kill me if her son wouldn't stop her? These, these are the people—the peddlers of hate. All we're doing is laying down our lives. We're not letting them take our lives. We're laying down our lives. Peace in their lives. They just want peace. (*Music.*)

MAN 5: All I would like to say is that my, uhm—my so-called parents are filled with so much hate—

JONES: (*Clapping*—not *applause.*) Stop this, stop this, stop this. Stop this crying, all of you.

MAN 5:—Hate and treachery. I think you people out here should think about how your relatives were and be glad about that the children are being laid to rest. And all I'd like to say is that I thank Dad for making me strong to stand with it all and make me ready for it. Thank you.

JONES: All they do is taking a drink. They take it to go to sleep. That's what death is, sleep. You can have it (*inaudible*) I'm tired of it all.

WOMAN 15: Everything we could have ever done, most loving thing all of us could have done, and it's been a pleasure walking with all of you in this revolutionary struggle. No other way I would rather go to give my life for socialism, communism, and I thank Dad very, very much.

WOMAN 16: Right. Yes, eh. Dad's love and nursing, goodness and kindness

28. Jim Cobb was one of the "Gang of Eight" who had defected in 1973. He was not, in fact, dead.

and bring us to this land of freedom. His love—his mother was the advance —the advance guard to socialism. And his love (*inaudible*) will go on forever unto the fields of—

JONES: Where's the vat, the vat, the vat? Where's the vat with the Green C on it? The vat with the Green C in. Bring it so the adults can begin.[29]

WOMAN 16: Go on unto the sing, and thank you Dad.

JONES: (*Inaudible.*) . . . Don't, don't fail to follow my advice. You'll be sorry. You'll be sorry. If we do it, than that they do it. Have trust. You have to step across. (*Music.*) We used to think this world was—this world was not our home—well, it sure isn't—we were saying—it sure wasn't.

He doesn't want to tell them. All he's doing—if they will tell them— assure these kids. Can't some people assure these children of the relaxation of stepping over to the next plane? They set an example for others. We said —one thousand people who said, we don't like the way the world is.

VOICE: Take some.

JONES: Take our life from us. We laid it down. We got tired. We didn't commit suicide, we committed an act of revolutionary suicide protesting the conditions of an inhumane world.
   (*Music.*)

29. The suicides were so well organized that the potion for the children was prepared in a different container (at a lesser strength, I assume) than the potion for the adults.

A Witness to Tragedy and Resurrection

*B*arbara and I were on a retreat last Sunday when I was called out of a meeting. I returned my sister's phone call and was told of the assassination of Congressman Ryan and the others. Mike and Foofie Faulstich brought us home. On the way, Mike said: "John, this is your calling." I knew what he was talking about.

We have been called to bear witness to the word God speaks to us now. I say "We," because you are as much a part of this as I am. There is no witness to the Word apart from the hearing of it.

Barbara and I are here by the love and strength of God which we have received through your caring and your prayers. I never imagined such a personal blow, but neither could I have imagined the strength that has come to us. We are being given strength now to be faithful to our calling.

I am a sponge. If my voice breaks or there is a long pause, I want you to know that it's all right. I am preaching this morning because we alone can make our unique witness, and today is the day to make it.

Following the sermon, we shall join in prayers of intercession for all of the people involved in this tragedy, from those first shot down to all who died, and all who grieve.

During these past days, we have been asked frequently: "How did your children become involved in Peoples Temple?"

There is no simple answer. We are given our genetic ancestry. We are given our families. We are all on our personal journeys. All of these, along with the history of the race, converge upon the present wherein we make

This sermon, which Rev. John V. Moore gave at the First United Methodist Church in Reno where he was serving as Senior Pastor, was delivered only seven days after the tragedy at Jonestown. The Scripture texts he used as its basis were Exodus 20:1–6 (the first and second of the Ten Commandments) and Matthew 25:31–46 (the Last Judgment).

choices. Through all of this, providence is working silently and unceasingly to bring creation to wholeness.

I will talk only of our children's personal histories. The only way you can understand our children is to know something of our family. In our family, you can see the relationship between the events of the sixties and this tragedy, just as there is a relationship between the self-immolation of some Americans during those years and the mass murder-suicide of last week.

Our children learned that mothering is caring for more than kin. Dad talked about it from the pulpit. Mother acted it out. More than fifteen teenagers and young adults shared our home with our children. Some were normal, but others had problems. One did not say a word for three months. At least two others were suicidal. One young man had come from a home where his father had refused to speak to him for more than a year. From childhood, our girls saw their mother respond to people in need, from unwed mothers to psychotic adults and the poor.

Carolyn loved to play, but as president of the MYF [Methodist Youth Fellowship], she pushed the group to deal with serious issues. She had a world vision. She traveled to Mexico with her high school Spanish class. Four years later, she spent a year studying in France. At UCD [University of California at Davis], she majored in international relations. As a member of the Peoples Temple, she stood with the poor as they prepared for and stood in court. She expressed her caring both in one-to-one relationships and as a political activist.

From 1963 until 1972, when Annie left home, Annie and Becky walked with us in civil rights and anti–Vietnam War marches. We were together in supporting the farm workers' struggle to organize. They stood in silent peace vigils. In high school they bore witness to peace with justice in our world. Their youth group provided a camping experience for foster children. When Annie was sixteen, she worked as a volunteer in Children's Hospital in Washington, D.C. She worked directly with the children, playing with them, playing her guitar and singing. The children loved her. She decided that she wanted to work on a burn unit, which she did at San Francisco General Hospital before going to Guyana.

Our children took seriously what we believed about commitment, caring about a better, more humane and just society. They saw in Peoples Temple the same kind of caring for people and commitment to social justice that they had lived with. They have paid our dues for our commitment and involvement.

The second question we have been asked is: "What went wrong?" What happened to turn the dream into a nightmare? I shall mention two things that were wrong from the beginning. These are idolatry and paranoia. I speak first of idolatry.

The adulation and worship Jim Jones' followers gave him was idolatrous. We expressed our concern from the first. The First Commandment is the first of two texts for my sermon. "Thou shalt have no other gods before me." Our children and members of Peoples Temple placed in Jim Jones the trust and gave to him the loyalty that we were created to give God alone.

It's not that they were so different from other mortals, for idolatry has always been easy and popular. The more common forms of idolatry are to be seen when people give unto the state or church or institution their ultimate devotion. The First Commandment says "No!" and warns of disastrous consequences for disobedience. The truth is that the Source of our lives, the One in whom we trust and unto whom we commit our lives is the Unseen and Eternal One.

To believe the First Commandment, on the other hand, affirms that every ideal and principle, every leader and institution, all morals and values, all means and ends are subordinate to God. This means that they are all subject to criticism. There was no place for this criticism in Peoples Temple.

The second thing that was wrong was paranoia. This was present through the years that we knew Peoples Temple. There's a thin line separating sensitivity to realities from fantasies of persecution. Jim Jones was as sensitive to social injustice as anyone I have ever known. On the other hand, he saw conspiracies in the opposition. I remember painfully the conversation around the table the last night we were in Jonestown. Jim and other leaders were there. The air was heavy with fears of conspiracy. The entire conversation on Jim's part dealt with the conspiracy. They fed each other's fears. There was no voice to question the reality of those fears.

As their fears increased, they increased their control over the members. Finally, their fears overwhelmed them.

The death of hundreds and the pain and suffering of hundreds of others is tragedy. The tragedy will be compounded if we fail to discern our relation to that tragedy. Those deaths and all that led up to them are infinitely important to us. To see Jonestown as an isolated event unrelated to our society portends greater tragedy.

Jonestown people were human beings. Except for your caring relationship with us, Jonestown would be names, "cultists," "fanatics," "kooks." Our children are real to you, because you know and love us. Barbara and I could describe for you many of the dead. You would think that we were describing people whom you know, members of our church. If you can feel this, you can begin to relate to the tragedy.

If my judgment is true, that idolatry destroyed Peoples Temple, it is equally true that few moments in our time have been more expressive of Jesus' parable of the Last Judgment of feeding the hungry, caring for the sick, giving shelter to the homeless and visiting those in prison than Peoples

Temple. A friend said to me Friday, "They found people no one else ever cared about." That's true. They cared for the least and the last of the human family.

The forces of life and death, building and destroying, were present in Peoples Temple. Death reigned when there was no one free enough, nor strong enough, nor filled with rage enough to run and throw his body against a vat of cyanide, spilling it on the ground. Are there people free enough and strong enough who will throw themselves against the vats of nuclear stockpiles for the sake of the world? Without such people, hundreds of millions of human beings will consume the nuclear cyanide, and it will be murder. Our acquiescence in our own death will make it suicide.

The forces of death are powerful in our society. The arms race, government distant from the governed, inflation, cybernation, unemployment are signs of death. Nowhere is death more visible than in the decay of our cities. There is no survival for cities apart from the creation and sustenance of communities within. Cities governed by law, but without a network of communities which support members and hold them accountable, these cities will crumble, and will bring down nations.

This is what made the Jonestown experiment so important for us. It was an effort to build this kind of common life. Its failure is our loss as we struggle against the force of death in our cities.

I have talked of history and our personal histories, of our journeys and our choices. Providence is God's working with and through all of these. God has dealt with tragedy before, and God is dealing with tragedy now. We are witnesses to the resurrection, for even now God is raising us from death. God whom we worship is making all things new.

Our Lord identified with the least of humans. Christ is present in the hungry and lonely, the sick and imprisoned. Christ, the love and power of God, are with us now. In Christ we are dying and are being raised to new life.

My last words are of our children. We have shared the same vision, the vision of justice rolling down like a mighty stream, and swords forged into plows. We have shared the same hope. We have shared the same commitment. Carolyn and Annie and Kimo served on a different field. We have wished that they had chosen ours, but they didn't. And they have fallen. We will carry on in the same struggle until we fall upon our fields.

No passage of scripture speaks to me so forcefully as Paul's words from *Romans*: "Nothing, absolutely nothing can separate us from the love of God we have known in Christ Jesus our Lord." This week I have learned in a new way the meaning of these words of Paul: "Love never ends."

Now may the Word which calls forth shoots from dead stumps, a people from dry bones, sons and daughters from barren wombs and life from the tomb, call you forth into the new creation.

References

Aidala, Angela A. 1985. "Social Change, Gender Roles, and New Religious Movements." *Sociological Analysis* 46, no. 3: 287–314.

Baird, Robert D. 1971. *Category Formation and the History of Religions*. The Hague: Mouton.

Bardin, David J., ed. 1994. *Psychological Coercion & Human Rights: Mind Control ("Brainwashing") Exists*. Washington, D.C.: Cult Abuse Policy and Research, 19 Apr.

Barker, Eileen. 1984. *The Making of a Moonie: Choice or Brainwashing*. Great Britain: Basil Blackwell.

———. 1986. "Religious Movements: Cult and Anticult since Jonestown." *Annual Review of Sociology* 12: 329–46.

Bednarowski, Mary Farrell. 1980. "Outside the Mainstream: Women's Religion and Women Religious Leaders in Nineteenth-Century America." *Journal of the American Academy of Religion* 48, no. 2 (June): 207–31.

Berger, Peter. 1967. *The Sacred Canopy: Elements of a Sociological Theory of Religion*. New York: Doubleday.

Biderman, Albert. 1962. "The Image of 'Brainwashing.'" *Public Opinion Quarterly* 26. 547–63.

Braude, Ann. 1989. *Radical Spirits: Spiritualism and Women's Rights in Nineteenth-Century America*. Boston: Beacon Press.

Bromley, David G., and James T. Richardson, eds. 1983. *The Brainwashing, Deprogramming Controversy: Sociological, Psychological, Legal and Historical Perspectives*. Studies in Religion and Society, vol. 5. Lewiston, N.Y.: Edwin Mellen Press.

Bromley, David G., and Anson D. Shupe. 1981. *Strange Gods: The Great American Cult Scare*. Boston: Beacon Press.

Bromley, David, Anson D. Shupe, and J. C. Ventimiglia. 1979. "Atrocity Tales, the Unification Church, and the Social Construction of Evil." *Journal of Communication* (summer): 42–53.

Brownmiller, Susan. 1975. *Against Our Will: Men, Women and Rape*. New York: Bantam.

Burrus, Virginia. 1991. "Naming the (Feminine?) 'Other': Heresy, Manicheism, and Sorcery in Late Ancient Christian Thought." Paper delivered at the American Academy of Religion, Kansas City, Kansas Nov. 1991.

Carter, Lewis. 1990. *Charisma and Control in Rajneeshpuram: The Role of Shared Values in the Creation of a Community*. Cambridge: Cambridge Univ. Press.

Chidester, David. 1986. "Michel Foucault and the Study of Religion." *Religious Studies Review* 12, no. 1 (Jan. 1986): 1–9.

———. 1988a. "Rituals of Exclusion and the Jonestown Dead." *Journal of the American Academy of Religion* 56, no. 4 (winter): 681–702.

———. 1988b. *Salvation and Suicide: An Interpretation of Jim Jones, the Peoples Temple, and Jonestown*. Bloomington: Indiana Univ. Press.

———. 1991. "Saving The Children by Killing Them: Redemptive Sacrifice in the Ideologies of Jim Jones and Ronald Reagan." *Religion and American Culture: A Journal of Interpretation* 1, no. 2 (summer): 177–201.

Eco, Umberto. 1979. *Travels in Hyper Reality: Essays*. Translated from the Italian by William Weaver. San Diego, Calif.: Harcourt Brace Jovanovich.

Feinsod, Ethan. 1981. *Awake in a Nightmare*. New York: W. W. Norton.

Festinger, Leon. 1957. *A Theory of Cognitive Dissonance*. New York: Row, Peterson.

Festinger, Leon, Henry Riecken, and Stanley Schachter. 1956. *When Prophecy Fails: A Social and Psychological Study of a Modern Group that Predicted the Destruction of the World*. New York: Harper and Row.

Foster, Lawrence. 1981. *Religion and Sexuality: Three American Communal Experiments of the Nineteenth Century*. New York: Oxford Univ. Press.

Foucault, Michel. 1972. *The Archaeology of Knowledge and the Discourse on Language*. New York: Pantheon Books.

———. 1988. *Politics, Philosophy, Culture: Interviews and Other Writings, 1977–1984*. Edited by Lawrence D. Kritzman. New York: Routledge, Chapman and Hall.

Freud, Sigmund. 1961. *The Future of an Illusion*. Translated and edited by James Strachey. New York: W. W. Norton.

Galanter, Marc. 1983. "Unification Church ("Moonie") Dropouts: Psychological Readjustment after Leaving a Charismatic Religious Group." *American Journal of Psychiatry* 140, no. 8.

Geline, Robert. 1978. "Nightmare in Jonestown." *Time*, 4 Dec., 16.

Hall, John R. 1987. *Gone from the Promised Land: Jonestown in American Cultural History*. New Brunswick, N.J.: Transaction Publishers.

———. 1995. "Public Narratives and the Apocalyptic Sect: From Jonestown to Mt. Carmel." In *Armageddon in Waco: Critical Perspectives on the*

Branch Davidian Conflict, edited by Stuart A. Wright, 205–35. Chicago: Univ. of Chicago Press.

Hatcher, Chris, 1989. "After Jonestown: Survivors of Peoples Temple." *The Need for a Second Look at Jonestown: Rememberg Its Peoples.* Edited by Rebecca Moore and Fielding McGehee. Studies in American Religion, vol. 41. Lewiston, N.Y.: Edwin Mellen Press.

———. 1992. Phone interview with author. 1 Dec.

Haywood, Carol Lois. 1983. "The Authority and Empowerment of Women in Spiritual Groups." *Journal for the Scientific Study of Religion* 22, no. 2 (June): 157–66.

Hoshor, John. 1936. *God in a Rolls Royce: The Rise of Father Divine—Madman-Menace or Messiah?* New York: Hillman-Curl.

Jacobs, Janet. 1984. "The Economy of Love in Religious Commitment: The Deconversion of Women from Nontraditional Religious Movements." *Journal for the Scientific Study of Religion* 23, no. 2: 155–71.

———. 1989. *Divine Disenchantment.* Bloomington: Indiana Univ. Press.

Johnson, Benton. 1963. "On Church and Sect." *American Sociological Review* 28.

Johnson, Doyle Paul. 1979. "Dilemmas of Charismatic Leadership: The Case of the People's Temple." *Sociological Analysis* 40, no. 4 (winter): 315–24.

Jones, Stephan Gandhi. 1992–93. Interviews with author. Marin County, Ca., 7, 11, and 19 Dec. 1992 and 25 May 1993.

Jorgensen, Danny. 1980. "The Social Construction and Interpretation of Deviance: Jonestown and the Mass Media." *Deviant Behavior: An Interdisciplinary Journal* 1: 309–32.

Kaufman, Debra Renee. 1991. *Rachel's Daughters: Newly Orthodox Jewish Women.* New Brunswick, N.J.: Rutgers Univ. Press.

Kern, Louis J. 1981. *An Ordered Love: Sex Roles and Sexuality in Victorian Utopias—The Shakers, the Mormons, and the Oneida Community.* Chapel Hill: Univ. of North Carolina Press.

Kerns, Phil, with Doug Wead. 1979. *People's Temple: People's Tomb.* Plainfield, N.J.: Logos.

Kilduff, Marshall and Phil Tracy. 1977. "Inside Peoples Temple." *New West Magazine.* July.

Kroth, Jerry. 1984. "Recapitulating Jonestown." *Journal of Psychohistory* 11, no. 3 (winter): 383–93.

Levi, Ken, ed. 1982. *Violence and Religious Commitment: Implications of Jim Jones's People's Temple Movement.* University Park: Pennsylvania State Univ. Press.

Lewis, Gordon K. 1979. *"Gather with the Saints at the River": The Jonestown Guyana Holocaust 1978.* Río Piedras: Univ. of Puerto Rico, Institute of Caribbean Studies.

Lincoln, C. Eric, and Lawrence H. Mamiya. 1980. "Daddy Jones and Father Divine: The Cult as Political Religion." *Religious Life* 49: 6–23.

MacDonald, Eileen. 1991. *Shoot the Women First.* London: Fourth Estate Limited.

Mills, Jeannie. 1979. *Six Years with God.* New York: A and W.

Moore, Rebecca. 1985. *A Sympathetic History of Jonestown: The Moore Family Involvement in Peoples Temple.* Lewiston, N.Y.: Edwin Mellen Press.

———. 1986. *The Jonestown Letters: Correspondence of the Moore Family 1970–1985.* Studies in American Religion, vol. 23. Lewiston, N.Y.: Edwin Mellen Press.

———. 1988. *In Defense of Peoples Temple—and Other Essays.* Studies in American Religion, vol. 32. Lewiston, N.Y.: Edwin Mellen Press.

———. 1989. *New Religious Movements, Mass Suicide, and Peoples Temple: Scholarly Perspectives on a Tragedy.* Studies in American Religion, vol. 37. Lewiston, N.Y.: Edwin Mellen Press.

Moore, Rebecca, and Fielding M. McGehee III, eds. 1989. *The Need for a Second Look at Jonestown: Remembering Its Peoples.* Studies in American Religion, vol. 41. Lewiston, N.Y.: Edwin Mellen Press.

Naipaul, Shiva. 1981. *Journey to Nowhere: A New World Tragedy.* New York: Simon and Schuster.

Nimmo, Dan, and James E. Combs. 1985. *Nightly Horrors: Crisis Coverage by Television Network News.* Knoxville: Univ. of Tennessee Press.

O'Dea, Thomas. 1966. *The Sociology of Religion.* Englewood Cliffs, N.J.: Prentice-Hall.

Palmer, Susan Jean. 1994. *Moon Sisters, Krishna Mothers, Rajneesh Lovers: Women's Roles in New Religions.* Syracuse, N.Y.: Syracuse Univ. Press.

Pavlos, Andres. 1982. *The Cult Experience.* Contributions to the Study of Religion, no. 6. Westport, Conn.: Greenwood Press.

Reiterman, Tim, with John Jacobs. 1982. *Raven: The Untold Story of the Rev. Jim Jones and His People.* New York: E. P. Dutton.

Richardson, James, Joel Best, and David Bromley, eds. 1991. *The Satanism Scare.* New York: Aldine de Gruyter.

Robbins, Thomas. 1989. "Reconsidering Jonestown." *Religious Studies Review* 15, no. 1 (Jan.): 32–37.

Robbins, Thomas, and Dick Anthony, eds. 1990. *In Gods We Trust: New Patterns of Religious Pluralism in America.* 2d ed. New Brunswick, N.J.: Transaction Publishers.

Robbins, Thomas, and David Bromley. 1992. "Social Experimentation and the Significance of American New Religions: A Focused Review Essay." *Research in the Social Scientific Study of Religion* 4: 1–28.

Rose, Steve. 1979. *Jesus and Jim Jones.* New York: Pilgrim Press.

Rose, Susan D. 1987. "Women Warriors: The Negotiation of Gender in a Charismatic Community." *Sociological Analysis* 48.

Sawyer, Mary. 1981. Manuscript, 1 Apr.

Shupe, Anson D., and David G. Bromley. 1980. *The New Vigilantes: Deprogrammers, Anti-Cultists, and the New Religions*. Beverly Hills, Calif.: Sage Publications.

Shupe, Anson D., and David G. Bromley. 1981. "Apostates and Atrocity Stories: Some Parameters in the Dynamics of Deprogramming." *The Social Impact of New Religious Movements*. Edited by Bryan Wilson. New York: Rose of Sharon Press.

Smith, Archie, Jr. 1982. *The Relational Self: Ethics & Therapy from a Black Church Perspective*. Nashville, Tenn.: Abingdon Press.

Smith, Dorothy E. 1987. *The Everyday World as Problematic: A Feminist Sociology*. Boston: Northeastern Univ. Press.

———. 1990. *The Conceptual Practices of Power: A Feminist Sociology of Knowledge*. Boston: Northeastern Univ. Press.

Smith, Jonathan Z. 1982. *Imagining Religion: From Babylon to Jonestown*. Chicago: University of Chicago Press.

Stark, Rodney, and William Sims Bainbridge. 1979. "Of Churches, Sects, and Cults: Preliminary Concepts for a Theory of Religious Movements." *Journal for the Scientific Study of Religion* 18, no. 2: 117–33.

———. 1985. *The Future of Religion: Secularization, Revival, and Cult Formation*. Berkeley and Los Angeles: Univ. of California Press.

Stoen Jones, Grace. 1992. Interview with author. Contra Costa County, Ca., 3 Dec.

———. 1992. Telephone interview with author, 7 Dec.

Thielmann, Bonnie, with Dean Merrill. 1979. *The Broken God*. Elgin, Ill.: David C. Cook.

Troeltsch, Ernst. 1931. *The Social Teaching of the Christian Churches*. New York: Macmillan.

Ulman, Richard Barrett, and D. Wilfred Abse. 1983. "The Group Psychology of Mass Madness: Jonestown." *Political Psychology* 4, no. 4: 637–61.

Weber, Max. 1958. *The Protestant Ethic and the Spirit of Capitalism*. Translated by Talcott Parsons. New York: Charles Scribner's Sons.

———. 1978. *Economy and Society*. Vol. 2, edited by Guenther Roth and Claus Wittich. Berkeley and Los Angeles: Univ. of California Press.

Weightman, Judith Mary. 1983. *Making Sense of the Jonestown Suicides: A Sociological History of Peoples Temple*. Studies in Religion and Society, vol. 7. Lewiston, N.Y.: Edwin Mellen Press.

Wessinger, Catherine. 1997. "Millennialism With and Without the Mayhem." In *Millennium, Messiahs, and Mayhem*, edited by Thomas Robbins and Susan J. Palmer, 47–59. New York: Routledge.

————, ed. 1993. *Women's Leadership in Marginal Religions: Explorations Outside the Mainstream*. Urbana: Univ of Illinois Press.

Willimon, William H. 1988. "Acts 7:54–8:3: Martyrdom of Stephen and the Persecution of the Church." In *Interpretation: A Bible Commentary for Teaching and Preaching Acts*, 64–67. Atlanta: John Knox Press.

Wilson, Bryan, ed. 1981. *The Social Impact of New Religious Movements*. New York: Rose of Sharon Press.

Wooden, Kenneth. 1981. *The Children of Jonestown*. New York: McGraw-Hill.

Wright, Lawrence. 1993. "The Sons of Jim Jones." *The New Yorker* 69, 22 Nov., no. 39, 66–89.

Yee, Min S., and Thomas N. Layton, with Deborah Layton, Laurence L. Layton, and Annalisa Layton Valentine. 1981. *In My Father's House: The Story of the Layton Family and the Reverend Jim Jones*. New York: Holt, Rinehart and Winston.

Other Sources

Federal Bureau of Investigation (FBI) Documents:

All references to FBI documents are from the Guyana Evidence Index, file number 89-4286 from the files of Carolyn Moore Layton and Ann Elizabeth Moore; these files were obtained through the Freedom of Information Act.

Peoples Temple Archives:

The Schubert Hall Library of the California Historical Society maintains the Peoples Temple Archives. The archives comprise three collections of documents that are referenced by box and file number. Each footnoted reference to specific documents includes both box and file number. The collection includes 130 boxes of documents compiled by the receiver of the Peoples Temple estate after the tragedy (MS3800); 12 boxes of documents taken from Jonestown, Guyana, by the U.S. government (MS3801); and 5 boxes of letters, photos, sermons, and other writings by the parents and sister of Carolyn Moore Layton and Ann Elizabeth Moore (Moore Family Collection). Recently, Stephan Gandhi Jones gave the Peoples Temple Archives many of his Peoples Temple photographs.

Index

Religion and Politics
Michael Barkun, *Series Editor*